SHRUBS&HEDGES

SHRUBS&HEDGES

Discover, Grow, and Care for the World's Most Popular Plants

EVA MONHEIM

Japanese spiraea
'Anthony Waterer'
(*Spiraea japonica*
'Anthony Waterer')

COOL
SPRINGS
PRESS

© 2020 Quarto Publishing Group USA Inc.
Text © 2020 Eva Monheim

First Published in 2020 by Cool Springs Press, an imprint of The Quarto Group, 100 Cummings Center, Suite 265-D, Beverly, MA 01915, USA.
T (978) 282-9590 F (978) 283-2742 QuartoKnows.com

Cool Springs Press titles are also available at discount for retail, wholesale, promotional, and bulk purchase. For details, contact the Special Sales Manager by email at specialsales@quarto.com or by mail at The Quarto Group, Attn: Special Sales Manager, 100 Cummings Center, Suite 265-D, Beverly, MA 01915, USA.

24 23 22 21 20   1 2 3 4 5

ISBN: 978-0-7603-6684-4

Digital edition published in 2020
eISBN: 978-0-7603-6685-1

Library of Congress Cataloging-in-Publication Data

Monheim, Eva, author.
Shrubs and hedges : discover, grow, and care for the world's most popular plants / by Eva Monheim.
LCCN 2019042458 (print) | LCCN 2019042459 (ebook) |
ISBN 9780760366844 (trade paperback)
ISBN 9780760366851 (ebook)
1. Shrubs.
LCC SB435 .M633 2020 (print) | LCC SB435 (ebook)
DDC 635.9/76--dc23

Design: Elizabeth Van Itallie
Front cover: Top: Janet Loughrey Photography;
    Garden Designer: Leslie Ebert. Bottom: Eva Monheim
Back cover: Eva Monheim
Photography: Eva Monheim, except by Louise Clark on
    pages 117, 118, and 119.
Illustrations: Mattie Wells on pages 50, 96, 97, 109, 113,
    114, 116, 120, 126, and 165;
    Karen Steenhoudton page 82, 86, and 90;
    Shutterstock on pages 31, 42, 43, 44, 45, and 47.
Printed in China

To Sarah, Andrew, Mohamed, Rachel, Stephen, and all my students.
Always follow your passion!

CONTENTS

A shrub-lined stream
bank at Chanticleer
Garden in Wayne,
Pennsylvania

INTRODUCTION

Shrubs, hedges, and hedgerows have long been part of my consciousness. My earliest recollections of these plants are from the neighborhood in which I was born. It was a new housing development near Philadelphia built on an old dairy farm in the early 1950s. There were older homes scattered around the edges of our development that dated back to the late nineteenth and early twentieth century. Across from our twin home of brick was an old stone- and asbestos-sided farmhouse with a giant hedge demarcating the boundary of the property. Looking back now, that house was a morsel of the rural life that no longer existed in our neighborhood. The land around it looked nibbled away—a remnant of its former self. There was also an old barn converted into a garage. Chickens, a dog, and a cat lived with the elderly couple who would pass on when I was still young, leaving a bygone era of an earlier America.

The giant hedge went on for an entire block. It ran along a small, narrow street that must have been a shady lane at one time. The hedge was trimmed once a year and then less frequently as the years passed. As the couple got to their final years, the hedge began to sag and bow outward and inward, like a moving caterpillar. The mouth of the hedge was a metal gate, and when opened, it led up a straight path to the wraparound porch. The hedge was privet, with its signature deep green color, and overhung with old trees to create a cooling effect in summer. On dark nights, the old home looked austere.

Toward the other end of the block sat another home, similar in age and style, with another wraparound porch. It too had a lush green privet hedge marking the property lines. Behind this carefully clipped hedge was a beautiful flower garden of roses and perennials. This home served as our local Unity-Frankford store where we could purchase almost anything for the family's needs. The owners had an old barn that was updated and painted in privet green and white—the typical colors of old farmhouses of the time. The big doors once opened for carriages to enter. On the side of the barn were old horse stalls, with Dutch doors that split in the middle so the horses could hang their heads over.

The privet hedges defined each of these properties, and with a depth of about 2½ feet (76.2 cm), they became habitat for chatty birds to rest and keep cool during the hot summer. In the late afternoon, when I would walk by the hedges on my way to the store, I could feel cool air on my legs. At the time, no one used the term *microclimate*, but that's what I was experiencing, thanks to the hedge border. When in bloom in late spring, the flowers were

Mountain Laurel (*Kalmia latfolia*) is a beautiful flowering shrub, ideal for shady to semi-shady areas of the landscape.

attractive to a myriad of pollinators and smelled thick and sweet.

My family also had a hedge behind our home, marking the boundary between us and the house that sat below. Our honeysuckle hedge was trained over a thick cattle fence, which created an entirely different boundary than the privet hedges of our neighbors' properties. The metal fence provided the framework for the hedge that spilled over the fence. It formed a soft, rounded arch, unlike the flat, sheared privet hedges. When the honeysuckle came into bloom, the hedge became a frenzied microcosm of insects pollinating the delightfully sweet, fragrant, tubular flowers. Butterflies, hummingbirds, bees, and other pollinators flew in from afar. The honeysuckle bloomed off and on all summer long.

We had a second hedge—a large rambling rose bush. The deep-red blooms appeared for 2 weeks in June, with a spicy fragrance.

During the summer months, I would sometimes spend time at my Aunt Helen and Uncle Paul's farm. The farm was over 30 acres (12 ha) and was parceled up by a series of hedgerows. Each field was planted with a different crop, and the hedgerows separated each crop from the next, with only a narrow opening to allow the tractor to pass through for planting, cultivating, and harvesting. The hedgerows here were made of various species of shrubs and trees. Along the base of the hedgerows were small flowering plants and groundcovers. These mini ecosystems were the remains of the ancient woods that once stood there, before the forests were cleared for farming. The hedgerows provided wind blocks and housed insect-eating birds and pollinating

insects. They were also home to many a fox, raccoon, and opossum.

Some of the crops were rotated between the fields—sweet corn, beans, squash, and numerous other crops, including strawberries. I remember my aunt telling us that we could go pick the huckleberries, blackberries, and blueberries growing along the hedgerow. Sour cherry trees, crabapples, wild roses, Eastern red cedars, red maples, and pin oaks also grew in the complex matrix of this mini woodland. Poison ivy, black gum, and white oak were residents in the long narrow woodland too!

The hedgerows were thick—about 8 to 10 feet (2.4 to 3 m) in depth along the narrow lane on which my aunt and uncle lived. There were no breaches between the road and field; this way, the valuable soils were protected from erosion. And the deep ditch along the roadway collected rainwater runoff, providing the hedgerow with ample water that slowly seeped down to the roots and eventually into the water table. The ditches were their own little mini environments of diversity, much like modern rain gardens. When there were huge storms, the water washed down the ditch and into the stream, which was the headwaters of the Little Neshaminy Creek. My aunt and uncle were farmers concerned with conservation, and it showed in the maintenance of the farm.

When the economic boom of the 1980s came along with massive housing developments, farms like my aunt and uncle's were sliced and divided—hedgerows destroyed and entire fields wiped clean of any living thing. Hedgerows disappeared, just as they continue to do in communities around the world in spite of their importance to the environment. The demise of the hedgerow has resulted in more runoff, dirtier waterways, and more dust in the air, not to mention the loss of the sense of place they once gave. Perhaps even more important is the loss of habitat and corridors for wildlife such as deer, fox, opossum, and other mammals, as well as pollinators, birds, and bats.

The protection of valuable resources like hedgerows cannot be ignored. Their importance to the environment is still not fully understood by developers and other entities anxious to have houses built for additional tax revenue. Only in more recent years have we begun to understand the invaluable services hedgerows provide for the ecosystem. Those that remain are even more precious than ever. Even the lowly hedge of my youth has been subjugated to plastic fencing that offers a sterile environment with none of the benefits of the living borders of the past.

Besides what was lost to development, we've also lost miles of hedging on old estates due to introduced pests and climate change. No matter where you live, if you look closely at the properties around you, you might find an old farmhouse that still has intact shrubbery. Lilac, flowering quince, an old-fashioned rose or two, and forsythia. Occasionally there may be a strip of growth, a salvaged remain of an old hedgerow.

The hedgerows and shrubs of the last century may still be found in small towns that were left to languish after bypasses were built for speedier travel. Old cemeteries may have some ancient plants that remain wildlife habitat and allow for the rediscovery of old cultivars of plants that were thought to be lost.

Can we ever get back the ecosystem services once provided by these plants? Through a conscious replacement of plants within our own gardens and communities, we can purposefully replant habitat, create new microclimates, and enjoy all of the other services these plants provide. Newer, more improved varieties of plants bring a renewed interest in what we've lost and remind us of everything we have to gain.

And diversity does not just have to come from a hedgerow. Nowadays, it can take the form of a beautiful garden that includes a plethora of shrubs capable of supporting the environment in many ways. Plant a wide array of shrubs to help temper climate change, to make new memories of picking berries with your children and grandchildren, to cut flowering shrub stems for someone's birthday, or to attract a rare bird that needs our loving attention.

It is my hope that *Shrubs & Hedges* inspires a new generation of plant lovers, future scientists, plant breeders, and plant hunters. And to help others love the same environments that inspired me to strive for fresher air, cleaner water, and cooler days. No matter where you live—in the wide-open countryside or in the most congested city—planting shrubs and hedges brings inspiration and benefits galore. And you'll be planting landmarks that generations of children will someday remember from their youth.

Shrubs create visual impact, while at the same time softening the harshness that has crept into our world. Plant shrubs and hedges to conserve energy, reduce noise, buffer strong winter winds, and help cool your pleasant place in the world. Lastly, plant to invite a myriad of wildlife that needs our support now more than ever.

CHAPTER 1

A PASSION FOR SHRUBS—THEIR GENERAL USES AND BENEFITS

Let's begin our journey with a look at what shrubs are, how we can use them, and what we have to gain by including more shrubs in our landscapes.

What Is a Shrub?

Shrubs are typically described as plants that have multiple woody stems, either at ground level or just above the ground with a shortened trunk. They can grow up to 20 feet (6 m) tall with ease. Large shrubs can also be shaped more like small trees, depending on how they are pruned. Shorter shrubs are usually given the name *subshrub* to distinguish them from their taller counterparts. Those shrubs classified as subshrubs are typically below knee-height.

Why Are Shrubs an Important Plant Group?
For Design Versatility

Shrubs sit below, at, and just above eye-level as we walk through the landscape; in essence, they are the eye candy of the plant world. In both their natural environments and in managed landscapes, shrubs exhibit many shapes and forms, purposefully fit-

ting into their environment like puzzle pieces. Rounded shrubs fit under the contoured arching branches of ancient trees at the woodland's edge, and vase-shaped shrubs create microclimates to protect native and non-native perennials growing snuggly beneath. Wide sprawling shrubs shield the soil below by rooting their branches when they touch the ground, all while providing habitat for small creatures. The human-sized scale of shrubs makes us aware that we are not just viewing the landscape, we are part of it.

In plantings, shrubs can be massed together using one species to form tightly clipped hedges or left to grow into their natural form, softened on the edges to develop blurred lines between the surrounding plant communities. Staggered plantings, with multiple species of shrubs combined together, allow for a varied visual effect that enhances dimension and form, whether it's along a border, flanking a walkway, or used as a backdrop.

In foundation plantings around buildings, shrubs reduce heat loss by blocking winter winds. They protect less cold-hardy plants from winter desiccation. They create

Sweet tea or gordlinia
(X *Gordlinia grandiflora*)

Below, left: Flowering quince has large blooms that are great for forcing for floral arrangements in late winter.

Below, right: The foliage of mountain laurel holds up well when used in floral arrangements.

multiple microclimates and offer winter interest when the bleak days of the season have taken their toll. Late-winter-blooming varieties nourish hungry pollinators after a long-frozen period and offer us an early taste of spring.

The possibilities are endless with the addition of shrubs. And make no mistake—these plants play critical roles when used to delineate a property line, hide a visual eyesore, or reduce the sound of a busy roadway. Their connection between the soaring tree canopy above and the ground-hugging plants beneath makes this plant group invaluable in natural landscapes and in designed gardens. Shrubs are the connectors of the plant kingdom!

For Soil and Wildlife Protection

Taller shrubs act as small trees while shorter shrubs take the position of a ground-cover, protecting the soil from erosion. Small, intricate shrubs act as protection for ground-nesting birds, rabbits, groundhogs, and insects. They are major food sources for larger mammals such as deer, moose, elk, and bear. Nut- and berry-producing shrubs allow for greater animal activity, and some are highly enriched food sources for us as well.

For Products for Human Use

Entire industries are created around shrubs because of the myriad of products that come from their plant parts. In the cut floral industry, large early spring-blooming shrubs, like flowering quince (*Chaenomeles speciosa*), are cut for forced blooming to create showy arrangements to herald spring, while evergreen and broadleaf shrubs are cut for their amazing and long-lasting foliage for use in floral designs, especially around the winter holidays. These shrubs include mountain laurel (*Kalmia latifolia*),

Right: Red twig dogwood 'Cardinal' can be woven into wattle fencing for the garden's border or laced into baskets. It also looks handsome against a green backdrop.

Far right: Winterberry 'Tiasquam' ripens early, and birds eat this before they leave on their migratory flights. 'Tiasquam' is also one of the taller winterberry cultivars at 10' to 12' (3 to 3.6 m), a hybrid introduced by Polly Hill Arboretum, West Tisbury, Massachusetts.

Bottom: Use five or six different winterberry (*Ilex verticillata*) cultivars or another berry-producing shrub in the garden to provide as much as six months of food for our avian friends. Winterberry 'Winter Red' provides later-season food for returning birds or birds that stay all winter. It makes great cut stems for floral arrangements too! (See Chapter 6.)

drooping laurel (*Leucothoe fontanesiana*), and cherry laurel (*Prunus laurocerasus*). Bare branches of red twig dogwood (*Cornus sericea*) can be used as structural elements in floral designs, as accents in the garden, as fencing materials, and for basket weaving.

Red twig dogwood can also be used to help stabilize streambanks and wetlands to prevent erosion. Chapter 10 takes a deeper dive into using shrubs to help mitigate water runoff issues and damage.

Spicebush gets its
name from the spicy
aroma given off by its
leaves and twigs.

For Migratory Bird Habitat and Food

Those of us who live in migratory flyways
will be amazed at the varied diversity of
bird species that will pop in for an early
morning breakfast or a late-afternoon
snack as they continue on their journeys
to their winter habitats or spring mating
regions. In a later chapter, I'll offer more
details on the importance of shrubs to migratory bird flyways.

For Edibles

Native spicebushes (*Lindera benzoin*) found
in our riparian (riverside or streamside)
corridors burst their buds early in the season with chartreuse blooms to announce
spring. Their leaves give off a delightful
spicy fragrance when rubbed between the
fingers. And when the leaves and twigs are
suffused in hot water, they make a tasty tea
that works wonders for coughs and colds.
Without this plant in our gardens, the
spicebush swallowtail butterfly would not
be able to complete his/her life cycle.

Other shrubs produce edible crops for
humans as well, including blueberries,
honeyberries, beach plums, elderberries,
gooseberries, currants, and many, many
more. Some shrubs are also enjoyed for
their flavorful nuts or seeds. And of course,
there are other shrubs that are used as
medicinal plants.

For Hedging and Privacy

The taller nature of some shrubs lends
them well to hedging for closing in an
area to create privacy rather than using a
fence. Sometimes a particular characteristic
makes a shrub more desirable for hedging
over another. For example, spines or thorns
deter intruders, and evergreens block noise
or an undesirable view. We'll take a deeper
look at using shrubs to create hedges in
Chapter 8.

For Pollinators and Other Insects

Chapter 9 takes a look at this very important use for shrubs. Many native pollinators,
including bees, butterflies, moths, beetles,
flies, and wasps, rely on shrubs as a source
of nectar, nesting habitat, food and forage,
and overwintering sites. In addition, a
broad diversity of other insects rely on this
valuable group of plants for sustenance and
shelter. Without insects, the food chain
would collapse, and shrubs play a valuable
role in protecting and preserving these
creatures.

Hedging of American arborvitae 'Lombarts' Wintergreen' (*Thuja occidentalis* 'Lombarts' Wintergreen') at Longwood Gardens, Kennett Square, Pennsylvania

The uses for shrubs, as well as the array of different types of shrubs, are endless. With that in mind, the primary focus of this book is to highlight shrubs that have a multitude of uses and have multiple seasons of interest. No matter your reasons for planting shrubs, selecting the perfect plants means that you'll create your own personal paradise filled with beauty, bounty, and benefits.

CHAPTER 2

ROOTED IN THE PAST— A SHORT HISTORY OF SHRUBS

Shrubs and mankind have lived hand in hand since the dawn of humanity. Shrubs have been a source of food and medicine for eons. The Bible mentions Adam and Eve covering their nakedness with fig leaves, and Moses sees God in the burning bush. The branches of shrubs have been used to crown kings and queens, victors, and scholars. They have also been used to make healing poultices for the ill and to conduct ceremonies for the living, the dead, and the newborn.

Let's look at a few of today's much-cherished shrubs and their role in human history.

The Rose

There are many important shrubs that have a long historical context, including the cherished rose. There are three stories about the famous Damask rose (*Rosa damascena*) and how it got from Syria to Europe. The first story reports that when the Romans built their colonies, they brought the rose with them, including to their colony of

---

Shrubs Used in Spiritual Worship

At the birth of Christ it is written that two of the three gifts given by the three wise men were frankincense (*Boswellia sacra*) and myrrh (*Commiphora myrrha*). Frankincense was considered at the time to be more valuable than the third gift of gold.

And even before the birth of Christ, myrrh had a long history of use in Egypt as an incense. It was believed to please the ancient god Ra when burned in the temples of worship. The shrub's valued sap helped forge the connection between man and god. Learning how to extract the precious sap to make incense without killing the plant was a miracle unto itself.

In Judaism, myrrh was used as a sacred anointing oil and was used to consecrate the First and Second Temples in Jerusalem.

Frankincense was gathered from the sap of a large shrub used in religious ceremonies as tribute to God and for healing the sick and honoring the living and the dead. Early Christian churches (Roman Catholic and Eastern Orthodox) used frankincense as part of the ritual of ceremony. And both myrrh and frankincense were used upon Christ's death to anoint his body. The cultivation of both frankincense and myrrh continues today in Oman and Somalia.

Catawba rhododendron
(*Rhododendron catawbiense*),
Jenkins Arboretum,
Devon, Pennsylvania

England. The second story states that the Christian crusader Robert de Brie of France brought the Damask rose back to France after the Siege of Damascus in 1147. And the third story tells of the rose being presented to Henry the VIII by his doctor in 1547. Although there were wild roses in England and other places in Europe and the American Colonies, the prized Damask rose was revered for its amazing scent and its connection with perfumery in the Middle East.

The importance of roses to the history of humans can't be overstated. With over 3,000 rose varieties in cultivation today, most of them in foreign countries, they continue to have close association with human health and well-being. Entire industries were built around the rose, including the soap, perfume, cosmetic, and culinary industries. In Iran, which was once ancient Persia, recipes handed down through the centuries use rose water or rose syrup as one of the important ingredients, particularly in pastries. Other places around the world have used roses as a food source too—including the American Colonies in their fight against scurvy and other health issues.

In the Roman Catholic church, according to St. Louis de Montfort, "The word Rosary means 'Crown of Roses,' which is to say that every time people say the Rosary devoutly, they place a crown of one hundred and fifty-three red roses and sixteen white roses upon the heads of Jesus and Mary. Being heavenly flowers, these roses will never fade or lose their exquisite beauty." The rose is synonymous with the Blessed Mother, and Roman Catholic Christians who had gardens planted a rose in tribute to the Blessed Mother.

The War of the Roses demonstrates the importance of roses in British history as well, with roses representing two royal households. The white and red rose were used as symbols for the House of York and the House of Lancaster respectively. The coat of arms of each household used the rose for its emblem.

During the French and English colonization period, roses were planted and cultivated in every new colony. Since that time, our love affair with roses in gardens and bouquets has continued both here and abroad.

The Camellia

Established in 1600, The East India Company began as an independent trading company to exploit trading in Southeast Asia and China. Tea (the leaves of a species known as *Camellia sinensis*) was their main import, but that wasn't all. The company funded plant exploration, which became a boon for Europe's wealthy plant collectors. In the American Colonies there were also

Damask rose
(*Rosa damascena*)

Japanese camellia
(*Camellia japonica*)

plant collectors who benefited from the East India Company's imports and exports, until the tea tax instigated the American Revolution.

The earliest-known camellias in Europe were in Portugal in 1550. They arrived there through Portuguese trading expeditions to Asia. But the arrival of the plant in England didn't occur until 1739. The decorative Japanese camellia (*Camellia japonica*) arrived in the United State at the end of the eighteenth century. Charleston, South Carolina, became the epicenter for production of this beautiful flowering shrub beginning in the early nineteenth century.

Camellias have the distinction of having over 300 species and over 3,000 cultivars that are still in production today. Plant breeding for hardier varieties and different bloom times helps drive the market today.

Shrubs with Edible or Medicinal Berries

Shrubs on the North American continent were first used by the Native Americans, who taught the European settlers how to use many of the medicinal and fruit-bearing shrubs. Pemmican, a lifesaving food made from berries, was made by Native Americans and also shared with French and English fur trappers. It could be stored for up to ten years. Pemmican balls or cakes consist of an animal meat—such as elk, deer, bison, or moose—thinly sliced, left to dry in the sun or over a fire until hard, ground, and then combined with equal parts tallow and dried ground berries. The berries could include blueberries (*Vaccinium corymbosum*), alder-leaved serviceberries (*Amelanchier alnifolia*), black chokeberries (*Aronia melanocarpa*), bird cherries (*Prunus avium*), or cranberries (*Vaccinium macrocarpon*).

Berries became a staple for the Colonial American diet in the summer months and were made into valued preserves for the winter. Today, blueberry and cranberry production continues to expand due to the health benefits of both.

The Lilac

Right: American cranberry (*Vaccinium macrocarpon*)—a subshrub

Opposite: Lilac (*Syringa vulgaris*)

The lilac (*Syringa vulgaris*) arrived in Europe in the sixteenth century through diplomatic relations between the Ottoman Empire and the Roman Catholic Church. The shrub later was introduced in the American Colonies in the eigtheenth century and written about by wealthy people of the time. The fragrant flowers of this shrub were used for soapmaking and in various toiletries. Numerous wealthy plant collectors had extensive collections of lilacs.

There are 900 clonal variants and cultivars of single- and double-flowering types today. The colors range from white, purple, and lilac to pink and red. There are bi-colors as well.

The Arnold Arboretum in Boston, Massachusetts, has an extensive collection of lilacs with 391 plants representing 180 different types. And the Barnes Arboretum at St. Joseph's University in Lower Merion, Pennsylvania, has over 150 different cultivars for public view.

The Azalea

In 1680, Asian azaleas (*Rhododendron* spp.) made their debut in Holland. The United States had their own native species of azaleas, but it was the Asian varieties that first took center stage for their evergreen foliage and colorful flowers. Asian azaleas made their way to the United States via England in 1848. The first hybrids were planted at Magnolia Plantation in Charleston, South Carolina, which later opened as a public garden in 1870. As the collections grew at Magnolia Plantation, azaleas were being grown in the north in greenhouses. By the mid part of the 1930s, azaleas were a mainstay in the east, with more cold-hardy varieties being bred and introduced. The cacophony of color was just what the country needed as it was pulling itself out of the Great Depression. People were hungry for cheerful colors in the garden.

Large estates like Winterthur Museum, Garden & Library in Winterthur, Delaware, had—and still have—massive collections of azaleas as the understory of their native woodlands. When the garden opened in 1951 to the public, azalea sales had already hit their stride across the United States.

Azalea hybridizing has continued up to this day, with new cultivars and hybrids on the market. The brand ENCORE® Azaleas has made huge inroads in the industry with its reblooming azaleas that offer greater interest in the garden year-round.

The Future of Shrubs

Many more stories about the history of shrubs could be told. Sadly, many of their histories have been obscured by the commonality of the plant in present day. An ordinary shrub today could have helped feed or medicate thousands in the past, but the story wasn't documented. Our botanic gardens and arboreta are extremely important as the record keepers of plant expeditions, discoveries, and new variations in species. Pressed plants or herbarium specimens from the original plants discovered are also housed in botanic gardens and become a huge database for research. They keep these valuable plants in front of the public's eyes.

The next time you are looking at a plant in a garden center, nursery, or big-box store, think about how that plant may have gotten into your hands. It may have been propagated for generations, and someone long before us may have protected it from extinction.

CHAPTER 3

HOW SHRUBS ARE NAMED AND HOW TO ID THEM

Now that you're familiar with the long and fascinating history of humans and shrubs, we'll turn our focus to why and how humans came to categorize, organize, and name the shrubs they grow and use. You'll also learn some tips for identifying shrubs in natural settings as well as in cultivated landscapes.

How Does a Plant Get Its Name?

Common names were the first names to be given to plants. Humans developed local names for individual plants so other members of their community would know which plant was which, and what each one was used for. Often plants were named according to how the plant looked or what function the plant provided. The same plant just a few miles away might be called by a different name because of how it was used in that particular community. Plants that had a similar function in multiple communities were eventually designated with the same common name.

For example, in the eastern United States, the shrub or small tree called serviceberry (*Amelanchier* spp.) also carries the common name juneberry or shadblow. The latter was the name given by indigenous peoples because there was a correlation

between the bloom time of the plant and the running of shad for spawning in nearby rivers. Fish were an important part of the diet of many indigenous peoples in the eastern United States, and the correlation between the two natural occurrences became inseparable. In other communities that were not reliant on fish for their diet, the shrubs were called juneberry. The name juneberry was a way to inform locals that the month of June was the time that the fruit was ripe. Instead of a calendar, time was marked by the natural cycles of living things. The repetition of these yearly events determined times of harvest, celebration, and thanksgiving. Many of these annual events are still defined in our heritage today, including, for example, the local shad festival along the Delaware River. Or the first appearance of local pies in the month of June at farm stands near juneberry and blueberry habitat. Most consumers have lost touch with the natural "calendars" of the past that were closely tied to the availability of certain foods, but they are reminders of how important plants were and are to our daily lives.

Serviceberry is found throughout North America, and in western areas it's known by yet another common name: saskatoon.

Serviceberry (*Amelanchier canadensis*), the peach-colored, multi-stemmed small tree in this photo

The word *saskatoon* was taken from the Cree people and dates back centuries. The berries from saskatoon were an important food source for native populations and were also used in pemmican (see Chapter 2).

In the case of serviceberry, there are no less than fifteen common names for the various species of the plant. You can be assured that if a plant has numerous common names, then it was and is an important plant for many different populations. These days, the plant is called serviceberry by most plant nomenclature authorities in the United States because of all the services that this plant has provided through the centuries. The main problem with this

Opposite: Inkberry
(*Ilex glabra* 'Shamrock')

Fact or Fiction?

There is another twist to the common name serviceberry. It may be an old wives' tale, but some believe that serviceberry got its name because when the shrub bloomed in the spring, the ground was thawed enough to bury a dead body after a cold winter. Since the ground was frozen solid in the winter, funeral services were performed en masse for all the bodies that had been waiting to be interred during the long, cold winter—hence the name serviceberry.

Common Names for This Book

If you are wondering how the common names are selected for this book, the Missouri Botanical Garden is the source of reference. Missouri has one of the largest databases in the country. It includes not just the plants they have in their garden, but others from around the country. If the plant name you're looking for isn't in the Missouri database, the Royal Horticulture Database for horticultural nomenclature is next in line. If that doesn't work, visit university websites such as the North Carolina State University plant database. You can also look to the USDA governmental website known as GRIN: National Genetic Resource Program. This website provides common and Latin names while also providing maps of plant nativity and range. As an aside, if you apply for grants from the federal government, you must use the GRIN site and their naming system.

---

standardization of common plant names is that often we lose our connection to the past and to the nuances of regionalism. The generalization of a single common name globalizes a plant, removing it from its original context, populace, and use.

In addition to assigning common names based on natural events, plants were also given common names based on their functions. For example, the small black berries of inkberry (*Ilex glabra*) were once pressed and used to make a high-quality ink. But, there were many plants used to make ink, so the common name of inkberry was assigned to those plants as well. With multiple plants being assigned the same common name, you can imagine the confusion that would arise when talking about a plant used for making ink.

Plants were also given common names for their healing properties. Other shrubs were named for their poisonous traits to warn of their fatal nature. And still others were named after what they could do. The common name of doghobble (*Leucothoe fontanesiana*), by way of example, warned people that their pets could get caught up in the massive thickets created by this plant along streambanks and low-lying woodlands in the South. Even people could get caught up in the mire of stems formed by the plant's growth pattern, while smaller animals were able to seek refuge in doghobble and hide from their predators. Today doghobble, with its interconnected branch pattern, is ideal for erosion control.

As I'm sure you can see from just these few examples, common names can tell you a lot about a plant. Unfortunately, these names have many shortcomings too. They are not a clear way to define one plant from

Doghobble (*Leucothoe fontanesiana*)

using a binomial (two-name) system. This was the first edition of Linnaeus's book, with many editions to follow. Formally organizing plants into categories is known as the study of taxonomy. Linnaeus worked in Sweden, Germany, England, the Netherlands, and France during his career, and he not only named plants in these countries, but he named animal species and rocks as well. He was considered one of the greatest scientific minds of his time. Linnaeus is known as the "father of taxonomy."

Delving into taxonomy is helpful for anyone who works with plants at home or intends to have a professional career in the horticulture or green industries. Understanding the basics can assist in identifying plants by their family, genus, and species. These three classification categories are discussed in further detail below, with the latter two categories comprising the binomial nomenclature system. In the box opposite is an example of one plant broken down to the species and even cultivar level.

Defining Family, Genus, and Species
Family

The first category that we'll examine is a shrub's *family*. The family is determined by the flower and fruit type that each plant produces, along with several other common traits. There are three forms of flowers that are found in the flowering plant world. The first is **a complete flower**, which is made up of male (or staminate) parts, female (or pistillate) parts, petals, and sepals. The second is **a perfect flower**. These flowers have both male and female parts but may be lacking petals and/or sepals. The third is **an incomplete**

another—especially between different geographical regions—and using common names results in confusion more often than not. Because of this, eventually scientists developed a universal nomenclature system to identify plants.

The Binomial System

During Roman times there was an effort to develop a two-name system for plants, but no formal nomenclature was ever established. It wasn't until the eighteenth century that we began to see the internationally recognized formal naming system that is still used today.

In 1735, Carl Linnaeus introduced *Systema Naturae*, a document that would forever change how plants were named by

Taxonomy Units

Sample plant: *Heptacodium miconioides* 'SMNHMRF' TEMPLE OF BLOOM®

Kingdom—Plantae
 Division—Magnoliophyta
  Class—Magnoliopsida
   Order—Dipsacales
    Family—Caprifoliaceae—honeysuckle family
     Subfamily—Caprifolioideae—subdivision of the honeysuckle family
      Genus—*Heptacodium*—*hepta* means seven, *codium* is taken from the Greek word "koidion"or fleece
       Species—*miconioides*—named after a small white long-tailed monkey from South America
        Subspecies—variation of the species, often called the *variety*
         Form or Forma—a plant found in the wild that typically does not breed true and therefore must be propagated asexually
          Cultivar—'SMNHMRF'—plant form put into production that is unique and different from other forms; names always appear in single quotation marks
           Legal Name—TEMPLE OF BLOOM®

Note: The legal name is not included in taxonomic naming, but I included it in my example to show the further development of naming that now extends outside of the existing scientific framework. Patents, trademarks, and registrations began in the United States in 1931 with the first patented plant, a rose. Globally, there are an enormous amount of patented and trademarked plants today. As a result, there is a special organization called the International Code of Nomenclature for Cultivated Plants (ICNCP) that oversees the naming of these plants. Trademarked and registered names are not a part of formal nomenclature.

(See page 212 for websites.)

FLOWER DIAGRAM

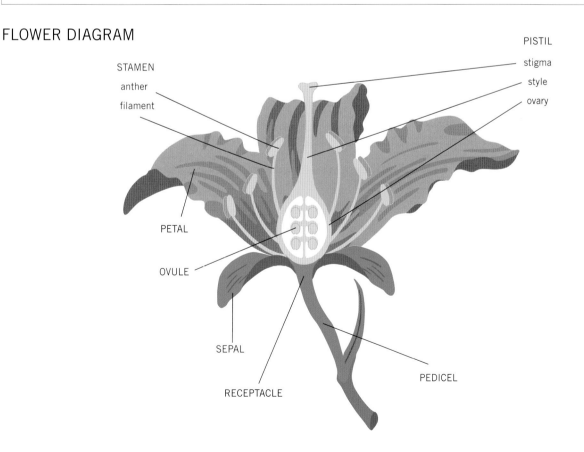

PISTIL
stigma
style
ovary

STAMEN
anther
filament

PETAL

OVULE

SEPAL

RECEPTACLE

PEDICEL

All in the Family

Flower structure is the primary attribute used to categorize plants into families. To give an example of two shrubs that share the same family, let's look at two popular members of the honeysuckle family (Caprifoliaceae), a family in which all members have tubular flowers. The seven-son flower (*Heptacodium miconioides*) produces a small white tubular flower. It has both male and female parts, as well as petals and sepals (making it a complete flower). When comparing seven-son flower to a plant known commonly as winter honeysuckle (*Lonicera fragrantissima*), they have an obvious likeness to each other. In addition to the same flower parts and shape, both have a sweet fragrance that attracts specific pollinators. This is another distinctive characteristic of many of the plants that make up the honeysuckle family. Although neither of these plants are in the same genus, they both carry the familial traits of the honeysuckle family.

▲ Winter honeysuckle (*Lonicera fragrantissima*)
▼ Seven-son flower (*Heptacodium miconioides*)

flower, which has either staminate or pistillate parts, but never both.

Plants within the same family have the same flower structure and share many other common traits as well. When naming families, each plant family was given a name that ends with "-aceae" and begins with a capitalized letter. Having a consistency in how the names were written created the framework needed for the continued expansion of the science. New plant family names continue to be added today as our understanding of plants continues to unfold. Sometimes plants are further categorized at the family level into subfamilies that share additional common traits.

Genus

The next level of nomenclature categorization is a plant's *genus*. When writing the scientific name of a plant, the genus name always comes first and is capitalized to provide clarity. The genus of a plant is determined by the presence of specific distinguishing traits within the plant's family (or subfamily, if there is one).

Species

The next categorization level below a plant's genus is its *species*. Technically known as the specific epithet, a plant's species clearly

defines it as separate from other plants within its genus based on its traits. The species name is written in lower case, and both genus and species are always italicized. Species is always subordinate to the genus. This is how all plants are written in documentation.

The genus *Lonicera*, as an example, has over 180 species within the genus. *Lonicera fragrantissima* is one of those species, so if I ask for that particular species at the garden center, I know exactly what I'm going to get.

Subspecies and Forms

A species is recognized as a plant that, when pollinated, will produce an exact replica of itself from seed, which is called *breeding true*. What does this mean? It means that the plant can reproduce itself over and over again and look the same each time. But every now and then a mutation can occur, especially when a plant has reproduced itself millions of times. The resulting mutated variation of the species can be yet another stable plant that is able to reproduce itself time and time again, producing the same new characteristics. When this happens, the variation is then called a subspecies because it too can breed true. The mutation could result in a different flower color, a unique leaf form, a size difference, shape difference, etc. The subspecies is always subordinate to species.

On rare occasions, different variations can occur that may not have the capacity to breed true (or even reproduce at all). In this case, the new plant then becomes categorized as a *form* or *forma*. In order for the new variant to be replicated, it needs help from propagators who reproduce the

Differences Between Genus and Species

An example I like to give students that helps them distinguish between genus and species is corn. If I send you to the grocery store and tell you to buy a can of corn, you can pick any can of corn off the shelf (level: genus). But if I say, bring back a can of whole kernel sweet white corn (level: species), then you must bring back a precise type of corn. Genus translates to speaking generally about a plant, while species means you are talking about a very specific plant.

plant by asexual means such as taking cuttings or using tissue culture to propagate the plant in a lab (more on shrub propagation in a later chapter). This anomaly of the species will disappear if the plant is not asexually propagated. There are many forms that occur naturally, and if they are not discovered by humans, the variant disappears when that plant dies. Many new plants are "discovered" this way. A natural mutation occurs that creates a new form of a plant. A human sees the variation as being desirable and decides to propagate and cultivate the plant for market. This is how many new plants wind up as cultivars in the marketplace.

Cultivars

Cultivars are plants that are unique to a species (or a subspecies or a forma, if one is present). They are put into production and are named by the discoverer or the breeder of the plant. A set of single quotation marks always brackets a cultivar name.

Diversity in the Landscape

Having numerous plants in the landscape that come from different families turns the landscape into a diverse ecosystem, even if the plants are not typically found growing together in nature. Having huge variations in landscape plantings ensures healthier plants and a healthier garden ecosystem, just as it does in wild spaces. There is a reduced likelihood of massive disease issues in a landscape with high diversity. Pests and diseases have different affinities toward particular plant families. The rose family (Rosaceae), for example, contains over 4,000 species. Because of the size of the family, there is a broad range of diseases that affects its plants. A small and ancient plant family like the ginkgo family (Ginkgoaceae) has only one family member—*Ginkgo biloba*. Over time, this plant family has distilled weaknesses from its genetic line, and as a result, its one remaining species has the ability to thwart

Right: Ginkgo (*Gingko biloba*) has many different forms. Ginkgo 'Todd' (*Ginkgo biloba* 'Todd') is a form of ginkgo that sits below the species on the nomenclature hierarchy. Ginkgo in its fall color—disease resistant, pollution, drought, and cold tolerant.

Far right: 'Todd' is the shrub form of ginkgo.

Sexual Interactions of the Intergeneric Kind

At the genus, species, and subspecies levels, plants have the ability to sexually interact with each other, with some plants being more fertile than others. There are plants that are incompatible with other plants, which makes cross-pollination difficult if not impossible in those cases. Crosses between different species within the same genus occur occasionally. And crosses between two different genera sometimes occur as well, but most often with the help of humans. This is known as an intergeneric cross. An example of an intergeneric cross is one between gordonia (*Gordonia lasianthus*) and Franklin tree (*Franklinia alatamaha*) that results in a plant known as sweet tea, or gordlinia (× *Gordlinia grandiflora*). *Intergeneric crosses* are noted with an × in front of the "Genus" and the result yields large flowers. In this case, the new genus name is a combination of the two "mother" genera. This particular intergeneric cross was created by Ranney and Fantz at North Carolina State University in 2003. Intergeneric crossed plants are replicated by asexual propagation methods (called *cloning*), most often through cuttings of the original plant, to ensure that each "daughter" plant will be identical to the original parent. Sweet tea or gordlinia has a greater hardiness than the original parent plant of gordonia because it was crossed with Franklin tree, which has a higher tolerance for the cold. The cross has a phenomenal red fall color and is classified as a large shrub or small tree. The flowers bloom in late summer through fall, giving a spectacular show. Intergeneric crosses are usually found in arboreta and botanic gardens first, before they are released to the public. Sweet tea is already making quick moves through the industry.

Left: Sweet tea or gordlinia (× *Gordlinia grandiflora*). *Right:* Franklin tree (*Franklinia alatamaha*) is one of the parents to sweet tea.

many of the ills that plague some other evolutionarily younger plant families.

Legal Plant Names and Their Complications

Naming has gotten a lot more complicated since Linnaeus began his system all those years ago. The race for the next best plant to hit the market and for naming rights to that plant continues to be a fascinating study. Today, what we see in the marketplace are typically common names with the legal branded names. The scientific names using the Linnaean system are usually located at the bottom front or back of the plant's tag. These days, legal branded names take priority over the Latin name in the marketing world. In order to sell plants, the trademarked name takes precedent to accommodate the marketing strategies to bring the plant to the public. The trademarked name remains with the plant through the entire marketing process. Most growers painstakingly develop their plant tags to give as much information as possible to the consumer, and the tags are quite costly to produce. Money derived from the sales of the plant always includes a fee for the breeder, the patent process (legal naming), and the cost of publicity and marketing, in addition to production costs and labeling. Plant patents are good for up to twenty years before they are no longer viable. Beware, however, because no patented plants may be asexually reproduced for sales by anyone other than the company that holds the patent or their licensed partners. You can only propagate them for your own garden use.

Patented, trademarked, and registered plants are a more recent development; the first patent was granted in 1931. Patented plants reside in a world of their own, with all the complicated legalities that go along with it, and their legal brand names sit outside the global rules of Linnaean nomenclature.

When writing a plant name that has a patent in the nomenclature world, it will be written as in the example below.

Scientific name—*Rosa* 'Radrazz'

Legal patent name—the Knock Out® Rose

DNA and Its Contribution to Nomenclature

On another level, with the advent of DNA testing, many shifts have taken place within the formal nomenclature framework. What was once thought to be a distinguishing characteristic for a plant placed in a certain family, genus, or species can sometimes be rebuffed by DNA testing. Testing may show that the plant in question shows a closer association to another species, forcing a reclassification of the plant.

We are in a wonderful age of greater refinement with taxonomy through the continued efforts of taxonomists around the globe. A good example of shifting nomenclature is in the genus *Viburnum*. This genus was once part of the honeysuckle family (Caprifoliaceae), but through new discoveries, it has been moved to the moschatel family (Adoxaceae).

Any major family shift or name change needs approval at the international level. The documents that guide name changes are found in the *International Code of Nomenclature of Algae, Fungi, and Plants* (ICN). A name can only be changed by the International Botanical Congress (IBC) with

Naming Cultivars and the Explanation of a Line

The Knock Out® Rose was developed by William Radler, a rose breeder from Wisconsin. He made many crosses of varying species of roses before he came up with the rose. That's why a species name is not listed. The first three letters of the cultivar name are the first three letters of William Radler's last name. The last four letters of the cultivar are from the original name that William Radler gave the plant—Razzle Dazzle. 'Radrazz' became the scientific name of the plant. There is a formality that goes along with this or any other cultivar: any further mutations (also known as *sports* or *chimeras*) that occur on 'Radrazz' will carry the first three letters of the originator's last name and then the first few letters of the last name of the person who finds the mutation. *Rosa* 'Radyod' Blushing Knock Out® was found as a mutation of the original 'Radrazz'. The gentleman who made the discovery of the soft pink rose was Mr. Yoder of Yoder Brothers, so the first three letters of his last name got added, giving us 'Radyod'.

A mutation that occurs from the original patented plant is called a line. A plant line can consist of many plants. In the case of the Knock Out® line of roses, there are eight plants and counting, each coming from the original Knock Out® Rose.

the support of the International Association for Plant Taxonomy (IAPT). In other words, when there is a name change, there must be a review of the request at a global level with supporting data and documentation from the institutions that support the name changes. More information on this topic can be found on the websites of the organizations mentioned in the Appendices.

The binomial system certainly helped clear up the confusion between plant common names. A plant might be called "poor man's bridal bouquet" in one part of the country, while in another place it's called "ninebark." The same plant in the binomial system has the name *Physocarpus opulifolius*. This Latin plant name is used universally around the world, even though people still have their common names for the plant. When you break down what the

Latin name means, you begin to see the characteristics in the plant and why it was named the way it was. *Physo* means inflate, and *carpus* means fruit. (See photo opposite.) *Opulus* means fancy or opulent looking, also taken from *Viburnum opulus* and *folius* means leaf in Latin. When looking at the plant, you see small inflated fruits with leaves that are opulent in form.

Technically, the Latin names are not all Latin, but a mix of ancient Arabic, Greek, and Latin. Other names come from the explorer who discovered the plant. *Malus sargentii*, for example, tells us that this species of the apple genus was discovered by someone with the name of Sargent. The double ii at the end of the name relates to the discoverer of the plant. Sargent was the first director of the Arnold Arboretum and went on many plant expeditions. He has many plant discoveries to his credit.

Below: Fuzzy deutzia (*Deutzia scabra*) was written about in 1781 by Thunberg as a tall vase-shaped shrub with exfoliating bark and prolific spring bloom.

Opposite, top: The American fringe tree (*Chionanthus virginicus*) flowers hang beneath the foliage.

Opposite, below: Chinese fringe (*Chionanthus retusus*) tree fruits sit above the leaves.

Authorship

The last area to be discussed in regard to nomenclature is a plant's naming through authorship. Authorship of a plant lies with the first written documentation of a plant. The first person to name the plant in an article in a professional scientific journal is the author. The plant's discoverer doesn't always align with authorship. Authorship lies in the botanical realm of scientific study and is the tag that appears after the formal naming of a plant. Let's look at the plant fuzzy pride-of-Rochester (the original common name), which is now fuzzy deutzia (*Deutzia scabra* Thunberg or Thun). *Deutzia scabra* was written about and, in this case, discovered by Thunberg. His article

appeared in the *Nova Genera Plantarum* in 1781. Documentation like this squarely becomes attributed to Thunberg.

The authorship after the name of the plant is usually abbreviated. In the horticulture trade, authorship is typically not listed, but should not be dismissed. It is extremely important to botanists. Kristina Aguilar, Plant Records Manager at Longwood Gardens in Kennett Square, Pennsylvania, mentions that sometimes plants can be authored in two different locations in the world. Who, then, is the true author? The person who published and introduced the plant first.

Shrub Identification
Morphology and Plant ID

In addition to standardized plant nomenclature, the science of morphology was developed to categorize and describe plants based on their form and structure. The morphology of a plant refers to the organization, arrangement, and design of its various parts. It's extremely useful when you're trying to identify a particular shrub or when comparing one plant to another. The aspects of plant morphology that tend to be most useful to gardeners are the vegetative and reproductive structures of a plant. The vegetative structures include the stem, bud, and leaves, while the reproductive structures include the flowers, fruits, seeds, or cones, depending on the plant. Let's start by looking at flowers and how their design and arrangement can help you identify a particular shrub.

Flowers and Fruits

When looking at flowers, the position of the flower creates a distinguishing feature for ID. The American fringe tree *Chionanthus virginicus*) has a distinct flower that hangs beneath the leaves in a fringe-like fashion. Conversely, the Chinese fringe tree (*Chionanthus retusus*) has flowers that sit above the leaves. These distinct differences help ID one species from another, though both are similar in many other ways. Both are wonderful small trees or large shrubs and are showstoppers in the spring when their blooms scream fringe festival. The flower fragrance of both plants is clean and sweet smelling, which is another ID feature.

Flowers can be solitary and found at the terminal end of the stems, or they can be axillary and grow from the base of the leaves. Flowers can also be grouped into inflorescences, which are groups of flowers growing together to form a more complex structure. Inflorescences can be in many forms, including spikes, corymbs, racemes, umbels, cymes, or panicles.

There are many other ways to look at flowers and their ID traits, but for all intents and purposes, the arrangement of the inflorescence gives enough detail to aid with ID.

Leaves and Stems

Looking at the morphology of a shrub's shoot system is arguably the most useful way to help identify it. Vegetative morphology includes factors like the arrangement of leaves on the plant's stem, how the leaves are shaped, the pattern of the leaf venation, and what the margin of the leaf looks like. Let's look at each one of these characteristics and discuss how they can be used to help identify shrubs.

There are many different shrub leaf forms that become more recognizable the

FLOWER STRUCTURES

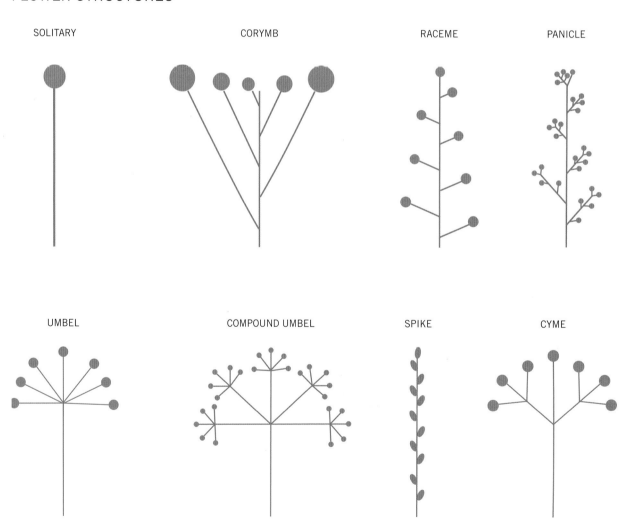

SOLITARY   CORYMB   RACEME   PANICLE

UMBEL   COMPOUND UMBEL   SPIKE   CYME

TYPES OF LEAVES

SIMPLE

PALMATE

BIPINNATE

PINNATE

more frequently you work with plants. Angiosperm (seed-bearing plants) leaves can come in various types, including simple, lobed, and compound. And there are even numerous types of compound leaves, depending on how the leaflets are arranged, including palmate, pinnate, and bipinnate.

Leaves can also have different types of margins, including smooth, serrated, or toothed. And they can be different shapes. Carefully examining the leaves for their many different features can help offer clues to the shrub's identity.

Even the way the veins are arranged in a leaf can help distinguish it from other species.

LEAF EDGES OR MARGINS

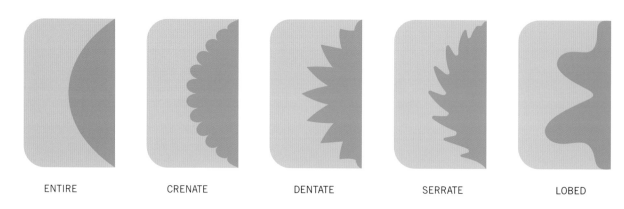

ENTIRE CRENATE DENTATE SERRATE LOBED

LEAF SHAPES

LINEAR ELLIPTICAL PALMATELY LOBED OBOVATE

PINNATELY LOBED RENIFORM LANCEOLATE

PATTERNS OF LEAF VENATION

| PINNATE | PARALLEL | PALMATE | CROSS VENULATE |

ID Features

Here is an example of leaf identification using red chokeberry (*Aronia arbutifolia* 'Brilliantissima'). First, the leaves are in alternate positions on the stem, see page 47. Then look at the leaves to determine what type of leaf is present (see page 44). In this case, red chokeberry has a simple leaf with a serration around the edge or margin. Once this has been established, you might notice hairy glands along the midvein of the leaf. Those hairy glands are a distinguishing feature of *Aronia*. From there, does it have red berries or black berries? If it has red berries, now you have narrowed it down to *Aronia arbutifolia*—red chokeberry. Both red and black chokeberry have hairy glands down the midvein of the leaves. If you are trying to determine the cultivar of red chokeberry, the fall color is the definitive factor. Viewing the plant in fall should reveal fire-engine-red leaf color. If it does, then you are looking at red chokeberry 'Brilliantissima'. The leaf on the cultivar usually has a slight sheen too.

All the ID features are present to make this plant red chokeberry 'Brilliantissima'.

Right: Hop tree's (*Ptelea trifoliata*) palmate compound leaf

Far right: The hop tree exhibits an alternate leaf position and lack of a terminal bud.

A good example of a compound leaf is the hop tree (*Ptelea trifoliata*). The leaflets are in threes in a palmate configuration. Note the veins on the leaflets; they are classified as pinnately veined (see page 45). This shrub or small tree grows well in a woodland or in full sun, and it has several other interesting characteristics besides compound leaves. It exhibits alternate leaves with an unusual trait of lack of a terminal bud. Instead, a leaf is in the place of a bud. Fruit is yet another identification feature that varies tremendously in the plant world. Hop tree has a wafer-like fruit that helps it fly or float.

The position of the leaf is another way to tell a plant's genus and species. They can be alternate as shown with the hop tree, or they can be opposite like viburnum, hydrangea, lilac, and others. A third leaf configuration is whorled.

The last example is the identification of a gymnosperm (cone-bearing plant). Members of the pine family (Pinaceae) have classic cones as we know them—pinecones that are used for decorating around the winter holidays. The leaves on plants in the pine family are classified as needles. Needles can be solitary on trees and shrubs found in the genera spruce (*Picea*), fir (*Abies*), or hemlock (*Tsuga*), or they can be found in groups, as with the genera pine (*Pinus*) and larch (*Larix*).

TYPES OF EVERGREEN FOLIAGE

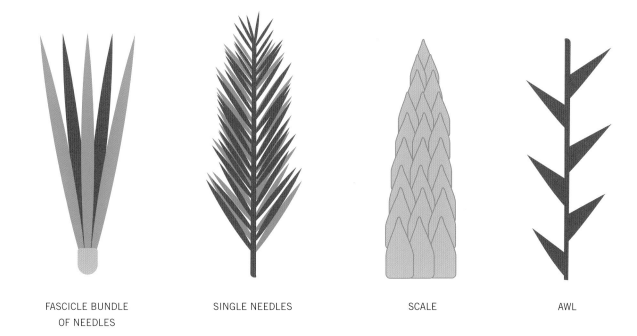

FASCICLE BUNDLE
OF NEEDLES

SINGLE NEEDLES

SCALE

AWL

LEAF POSITIONS

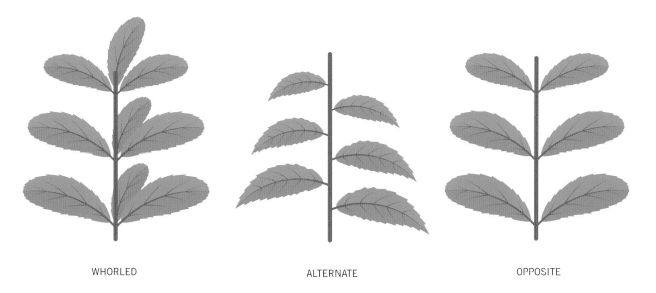

WHORLED

ALTERNATE

OPPOSITE

Right: Weeping Norway spruce (*Picea abies* 'Pendula')

Below: The cones on Norway spruce are easily identified by their triangle-shaped scales that are toothed on the tip.

Opposite, left: Both scale and awl foliage hanging in thread-like appearance

Opposite, top right: Gold-threaded Japanese falsecypress (*Chamaecyparis pisifera* 'Filifera Aurea')

Opposite, bottom right: Berry-like cones of gold-threaded Japanese falsecypress

When studying the cypress family (Cupressaceae), the foliage is made of two types of structures—scales and awls (see page 47). The scale foliage looks as though it is overlapping, and the foliage can take numerous positions and forms. The awl-shaped foliage gets its name from the tool used for punching holes in leather. One shrub that exhibits both scale and awl foliage is gold-threaded Japanese falsecypress (*Chamaecyparis pisifera* 'Filifera Aurea'). Foliage from this plant family is considered fine or very fine in texture and provides a range of visuals in the garden landscape. The forms of the plants can be beautiful and, for the most part, should rarely be pruned so as not to destroy their natural beauty.

HOW SHRUBS ARE NAMED AND HOW TO ID THEM 49

SHAPE AND FORM

UPRIGHT-ROUNDED

PROSTRATE-SPREADING

FOUNTAIN OR VASE-LIKE

ROUNDED

FASTIGIATE / COLUMNAR

PENDULOUS OR WEEPING

Overall Plant Structure

Another trait to be considered when it comes to IDing a shrub is the overall shape and form of the plant. Are the branches arching or upright? Is the plant rounded or vase-shaped? Does it hug the ground or stand straight and stiff?

Once you have learned to examine these traits and use them to assist you in shrub ID, an entirely new world of understanding will open up for you. You will find yourself selecting a greater variation of plant shapes, flower types, leaf forms, colors, and textures for your landscape or for plantings you take care of if you're a professional in the industry. There are many excellent shrub ID books to aid you in the process. The most important takeaway from plant ID, of course, is to have fun doing it. Make it a game.

Characteristics That Help Identify Shrubs and Other Plants

- **Branching Habit**
—Alternate
—Opposite
—Whorled

- **Bud**
—Shape
—Form

- **Bark Characteristics**
—Deeply furrowed
—Mottled
—Exfoliating
—Distinguishing color/colors

- **Leaf Characteristics**
—Leaf versus needle
—Shape
  Vein structure
—Deciduous, evergreen, semi-evergreen

- **Flower Characteristics**
—Complete
  Perfect
—Imperfect

- **Overall Shape of the Plant**
—Pyramidal and/or conical
—Columnar
—Spreading
—Globus/round
—Pendulus/weeping

- **Distinguishing Color of Any of the Parts**
—Solid
—Mottled
—Variegated

- **Distinguishing Fragrance**
—Aminoid
—Heavy
—Aromatic
—Violet
—Rose
  Lemon

CHAPTER 4

PROFILES OF DEPENDABLE CLASSICS AND RISING STARS

I f you've never gardened before, it may be a daunting task to select shrubs that will thrive in your garden. How do you know what to pick? How big will the plant get? What color flowers will the plant have? Is the plant dependable? In this section, we will take the mystery out of these questions with a look at how shrubs get to market and what breeders and plant explorers are looking for when selecting plants for the public.

New Releases

Each year there are a multitude of new shrubs introduced in the marketplace. But before new plants are brought onto the market, companies test these plants and have them withstand two or three winters in the field to see if there are any negative consequences during exceptionally cold winters, including breakage under heavy snow loads. In the summer, they monitor the heat tolerance of the shrubs, as well as resistance to drought conditions and heavy rainstorms. The plants are not pampered or fussed over in the field in order to simulate the homeowner's lack of attention. After the first trials, shrubs are sent out to a broad array of nurseries, botanic gardens, arboreta, universities, and garden communicators to see how they'll tolerate various climates. Shrubs are assessed for disease and insect resistance, fruit set, the aggressive or non-aggressive nature of the seed, the color and longevity of bloom, pollinator attractiveness, growth rate, and any other specific trait that may be desirable to the consumer's eye. Once the plants are in the hands of the gardener, there should be very few issues. A satisfied client will consider purchasing again and again when other new plants come on the market.

The research behind each plant also guarantees a certain level of performance without the use of pesticides. Breeders and nurseries have been gearing up for safer environmental conditions for years, and they have considered climate change too! Their commitment to the consumer goes far beyond the point of sale. For production, many companies have shifted to organic methods of growing, ensuring safe methods for the environment while delivering a top-quality product to the consumer.

But the testing of plants does not stop once the consumer has the plant in hand. Why? Because of our ever-changing climate, breeders and growers must stay ahead of the curve in order to make sure that the market contains a huge array of plant

Bigleaf hydrangea
'Tokyo Delight'
(*Hydrangea macrophylla*
'Tokyo Delight')

species that can endure environmental changes. Plant testers will look at plants again as time goes on to see if they are still performing to the original standards, even after the plants have been on the market for quite some time. Various organizations, botanic gardens, universities, and arboreta appraise the value of a shrub or tree and deem it exceptional if it continues to perform as it did when it was first released. The Pennsylvania Horticultural Society, University of Georgia, Missouri Botanical Garden, and Charleston Horticultural Society all have similar plant evaluation programs. The Royal Horticultural Society has a comparable program called Award of Garden Merit (AGM), which currently recognizes 7,000 plants out of the 100,000 that are grown in the United Kingdom. The AGM assures consumers they are getting plants that will consistently perform well in their British gardens.

Consumers Help in the Process

Consumers add another layer of evaluation. If one consumer finds the plant easy to grow, then other consumers may be more likely to try it as word spreads. As with other industries, word-of-mouth endorsements are the most effective way for a plant to maintain its status.

Testing takes a great deal of money in addition to the patent fees, publicity, and marketing that go along with releasing a new plant. There is also the fee paid to the person who discovered the plant in the wild or to the plant breeder who took years to develop the plant. Patented and trademarked plants require hundreds of thousands of dollars in publicity and marketing to get the shrub to a national audience through third-party endorsements. This form of "getting-the-word-out" takes time and patience, and with patents and trademarks, each plant sold carries a royalty fee that goes back to the breeder or the discoverer. The entire process is fascinating and is certainly a topic for another book. Plant marketing is an amazing profession, and it is most gratifying once the plant has the nod from the consumer. It makes the entire process worth all the effort.

Despite the multitude of plants brought to market, there are large numbers of plants that never make it to market. If the nursery or plant company making the release doesn't have the money to complete the process, the plant can sit in arboreta and botanic gardens for years unnoticed, even though it may be a great performer.

If a plant is a tried-and-true performer but doesn't work in your garden, don't feel bad. There are always a certain percentage of plants that don't work for a specific gardener because of unforeseen circumstances, often within the garden itself. Be assured that every gardener will lose plants due to freak storms, late-season frost, lack of water, or unexpected soil issues like poor drainage. Gardening is an art and a science, and experimentation is a huge part of it. The consumer may even discover something about a plant that wasn't known before. Sharing the information with your garden center or other plant organization can be helpful. See plant organization list in the appendix, page 212.

Left: Rhododendron
'Olga Mezitt'
(*Rhododendron* (PJM
Group) 'Olga Mezitt')
with its spring bloom

Right: Winter foliage
of Rhododendron
'Olga Mezitt'

Where Do Shrubs Come From?

Where do our new plants come from on the market today? They may come from older plants that were in vogue in the last century and are being rediscovered by nursery staff and breeders in arboreta or on old estates. Sometimes plantspeople will go into the wild (at certain sites with permission and licensing) and seek out new variations of a species. A good example of this is plant hunting in China, where there are many species of rhododendron that have never been seen before outside of that country. Seeds are collected and brought back to the United States—with all the proper paperwork—and are planted out in the field to see what germinates from the collection. Once germinated, some plants can be different in flower color, size, and shape. If there is nothing on the market like these shrubs, and they pass the test of time with consistent performance, the plants will be released after years of evaluations. Or a breeder can try to breed a shrub that is

hardier and more disease-resistant than the species. A good example of this form of breeding are the PJM rhododendrons (*Rhododendron* (PJM Group)) that were bred in the 1930s and 1940s. The plants were developed by the owners of Weston Nurseries in Massachusetts. Peter John Mezitt (PJM) and his son Edmund were looking for smaller-statured rhododendrons that would provide an array of bloom while enduring the cold winters in Massachusetts and the upper tier of the United States. They made many crosses, and when the plants began to bloom, Peter was certain they were onto something. 'Olga Mezitt'—named after Peter's wife—is displayed in the photograph above. The winter foliage turns a deep burgundy, with the oldest leaves turning red in late fall. This cultivar consistently blooms in profusion each year because it has sterile flowers.

There are plants that were popular almost a century ago that have gone off the radar or were never brought into the

Japanese kerria
cascading over
a stone wall

industry for propagation. They may be hiding in plain view in a botanic garden or in a private garden, but they don't have a good public relations team. When an old plant is "rediscovered," it's like finding a new plant. It may be put into cultivation right away or put into a breeding program to produce new cultivars that have different desirable attributes, such as leaf and flower colors or a new size and shape.

Plants also follow the fashion industry. Did you ever notice that the color of the year just happens to be one of the top-selling flower colors in the marketplace?

It's not by accident. Plants follow fashion and fashion follows the plant industry, along with other industries like paints, fabrics, and furnishings. The colors in the garden match the decor of the home and vice versa. All of these aspects come into play when breeders are looking for the next best plant—always keeping in mind the plant's performance.

Great Performers for the Garden: Shrub Profiles

The plants in the next section of this chapter are broken down by seasonal interest to help you add color and texture to your garden year-round. These profiles are just a small fraction of the plants that are available in the marketplace, but they are some of my personal favorites. My aim is to encourage you to explore and experiment with some of these wonderful shrubs.

Spring Couture

Spring is the time when the plant world wakes up and gives us gardeners the display of a lifetime. From soft pastels to bold colors, you'll want shrubs that scream spring.

Japanese rose or kerria (*Kerria japonica* 'Pleniflora')

The double form of the Japanese kerria 'Pleniflora' (this cultivar is sterile) is a tough plant that's best sited in a partially shaded, well-drained area. It typically grows along high stream banks in its native habitat in Japan and China. Poorer soils yield more blooms, while richer soils yield more stem and leaf growth. Ideal places to plant Japanese kerria are in perennial borders, in hedgerows, and as a focal point in foundation plantings. The plant has a graceful appearance year-round, with bare green stems during the winter months. In the summertime, it has pure-green leaves. The heaviest yellow-orange bloom occurs in spring, but this shrub may bloom sporadically throughout the summer. Flowers in their single form are found on another cultivar called 'Superba'. The single flowers of 'Superba' have five petals, a distinguishing trait of the rose family (Rosaceae). Kerria was introduced to the United States in 1834. Later, it became common on large estates through the mid part of the twentieth century. The Japanese kerria is ripe for a revival, with several new cultivars waiting in the wings. If you have a hard-to-mow slope or a shady location that receives morning sun, consider planting Japanese kerria. It looks beautiful when combined with underplantings of groundcovers and shade-loving perennials that bloom throughout the summer. Add some fall-blooming bulbs for a dramatic effect and a full year's worth of interest. The arching branches of kerria also look great cascading over a wall.

Height: 3'–6' (0.9–1.8m)
Width: 6'–9' (1.8–2.7m)
Cold Tolerance: -20°F (-29°C)
Seasons of Interest: All Seasons
Lighting Requirements: Partial Shade–Morning Sun

Dwarf fothergilla (*Fothergilla gardenii*)

With summer leaves that range in color from deep moss-green to blue-green depending on the cultivar, dwarf fothergilla has fabulous fall foliage in yellow to red. Its overall shape is rounded, but it will form colonies from sucker growth. The slow growth rate means no pruning is

necessary, which is ideal to reduce overall maintenance. It's best known for its beautiful white bottlebrush-like spring flowers, which emerge early before the leaves. The fabulously fragrant flowers make the plant ideal close to entryways. Dwarf fothergilla prefers acidic, well-drained soil and does well in full sun or partial shade. And it has a reputation for being a trouble-free native plant. Here are some good performers—'Jane Platt', 'Suzanne', and 'Blue Mist'. There are also wonderful hybrids (crosses between two separate species), including 'Mount Airy', 'Blue Shadow', 'KLMfifteen' Red Monarch™, and 'Windy City'. Look for more plants in this genus in the next few years.

Height: 1½'–3' (46–90 cm)
Width: 2'–4' (0.6–1.2 m)
Cold Tolerance: -10°F (-23°C)
Seasons of Interest: Spring–Fall
Lighting Requirements: Full Sun–Part Shade

Slender deutzia

Slender deutzia (*Deutzia gracilis*)

This shrub is a comeback kid after being an old estate plant in the last century. The resurgence not only includes the species, but two stars in the industry—'Nikko' and 'Duncan' CHARDONNAY PEARLS®. These slender deutzias have white flowers, but there are pink flower forms too!

CHARDONNAY PEARLS® has lovely chartreuse foliage that brings a brightness to a dull garden area. It was released in the industry in 2005 and is finally getting the applause that it deserves. The species,

like the two cultivars, has a rounded or mounded habit, with the species being the tallest of the lot. The bright green leaves of the species and 'Nikko' make them crisp and clean looking, especially when topped with their beautiful white flowers in April to May. You can prune lightly directly after bloom so the seed heads don't remain during the winter. Or you don't have to prune it at all. The flowers are clustered in racemes that provide a wonderful fragrance for about 2 weeks. The shrubs can be planted in full sun (or partial shade so the flowers don't fry on the occasional hot spring day). These plants are slow growers—a hands-off strategy is best. This group of plants always looks perfect in the garden setting and grows in a range of pH and soils, including clay. I have a feeling there will be more coming from this group soon.

Height: 2'–5' (0.6–1.5 m)
Width: 2'–5' (0.6–1.5 m)
Cold Tolerance: -10°F (-23°C)
Seasons of Interest: Spring–Fall
Lighting Requirements: Full Sun–Part Shade

Bridal wreath spiraea (*Spiraea prunifolia* 'Plena')

This is the double flower form. Variety *Simpliciflora* is the single white flower form and is rarely grown commercially. Another old estate plant, bridal wreath spiraea gets its common name because the stems can be made into beautiful bridal headpieces for weddings—it resembles baby's breath (*Gypsophila paniculata*). The flowers are sterile and appear before the foliage, emphasizing the flowers and their delicate nature. The cut stems hold up well in vase arrangements. Besides its amazing white bloom in spring, the fall color is vibrant as well, in deep oranges and reds. Ideal for hedging, borders, naturalized areas, or as a specimen, it tolerates a wide range of soils and is drought tolerant. There is no need to prune this shrub. Bridal wreath's original nativity is Korea and China, and it was introduced to the United States during the Civil War in 1864.

Height: 4'–8' (1.2– to 2.4 m)
Width: 4'–8' (1.2–2.4 m)
Cold Tolerance: -10°F (-23°C)
Seasons of Interest: Spring–Fall
Lighting Requirements: Full Sun–Part Shade

Bridal wreath spiraea

Cutleaf lilac (*Syringa × laciniata*) at Ambler Arboretum, Ambler, Pennsylvania

Cutleaf lilac (*Syringa × laciniata*)

The leaves of this beautiful shrub begin with an entire edge or leaf margin and then slowly, as the leaves age, transform to heavily lobed leaves that resemble lace (hence the species name laciniata). The plant is believed to be a cross between common lilac (*Syringa vulgaris*) and Persian lilac (*Syringa × persica*). It has delicate flowers and a sweet fragrance that attracts tons of pollinators. Cutleaf lilac is an introduction from China. Its habit is a wide stature that is shorter in height. It is highly heat tolerant—a great plant for siting in the city with ample room. The genus *Syringa* has twelve species recognized, and there are many new plants coming out from the species and their crosses, including the BLOOMERANG® series, which are rebloomers. The sizes range from 1½ feet (46 cm) to over 12 feet (3.6 m)—there's a lilac for every garden.

Height: 4'–5' (1.2–1.5 m)
Width: 4'–5' (1.2–1.5 m)
Cold Tolerance: -20°F (-29°C)
Seasons of Interest: Spring–Fall
Lighting Requirements: Full Sun

Fetter bush (*Leucothoe racemosa*)

This shrub has been going through some name changes, and you may see it listed as *Eubotrys racemosa*, especially on governmental websites. It's perfect for streambank sites—its roots have strong stabilizing abilities to prevent erosion during heavy rains. A native from Maine to Florida, the small white flowers that appear at the ends of the branches are in stalks or racemes. The flowers have a sweet fragrance, hence its other common name—sweetbells. Bloom time occurs from April to June. The shrub likes acidic soils and moist conditions, prefers to be out of windy sites, and doesn't have a tolerance for drought. If you are planting fetter bush in full sun, make sure the soil doesn't dry out. The fall foliage display ranges from yellow to red before it nods off to sleep for the winter—no maintenance necessary except for an occasional pruning of the three Ds (see Chapter 6). Fetter bush is ready to take the native plant market by storm for rain gardens and riparian plantings, and to attract an array of pollinators.

Above: Fetter bush (*Leucothoe racemosa*) on the edge of a wetland

Below: The beautiful flower of the Oyama magnolia

Height: 3'–8' (0.9–2.4 m)
Width: 2'–4' (0.6–1.2 m)
Cold Tolerance: -10°F (-23°C)
Seasons of Interest: Spring–Fall
Lighting Requirements: Full Sun–Part Shade

Oyama magnolia (*Magnolia sieboldii*)

The Oyama magnolia flies under the radar for many plant lovers. It's classified as a shrub rather than a tree like the majority of magnolias. Compared to other Asian magnolias, Oyama typically leafs out first and then blooms in a similar fashion to the American native magnolias. The leaves are the backdrop for the unique blooms. The flower buds resemble eggs that are pointy, with a fuzzy (tomentose) covering. They position themselves almost horizontally before opening, and after opening, they hang their heads downward as if in prayer. The pure white blooms and crimson stamens on the inside of the cup-shaped flower are best viewed from below. If this magnolia is planted on a slight incline, you will be able to view the flowers from beneath and enjoy the lovely fragrance and beautiful interior. The flowers appear May through July, and prefer a partially shaded retreat with nice moist soil to provide the best bloom possible.

An interesting historical fact: around the time of the Civil War there were numerous plant expeditions to Asia by plant hunters from the United States, and the Oyama magnolia was one plant that made it back in 1865. It has been waiting for its stardom ever since. The name Oyama comes from the city's name in Japan close to where it was found.

Height: 10'–15' (3–4.6 m)
Width: 10'–15' (3–4.6 m)
Cold Tolerance: 0°F (-18°C)
Seasons of Interest: Spring–Fall
Lighting Requirements: Full Sun–Part Shade

Koreanspice viburnum (*Viburnum carlesii* 'Compactum')

This species was first brought to the United States from Korea in 1812, when wars were raging. In 1953, 'Compactum' appeared in the trade. It was in the 1980s and 1990s that several newer cultivars were introduced, and the plant has been on

Above: Koreanspice viburnum flower (*Viburnum carlesii* 'Compactum')

Right: Korean rhododendron (*Rhododendron mucronulatum*)

an upward trend since. There were several new cultivars released at the turn of this century, and I do believe the plant is here to stay. Koreanspice viburnum has a dreamy, sweet, spicy fragrance in the spring emanating from the clusters (cymes) of tubular flowers that start out pink when in bud and open to a pure white. Once the flowers are done blooming sometime in May, the fruit starts to develop into small egg-shaped drupes. These fruits start out green, then turn red, then become black-blue when fully ripe. There is no need to do anything to this plant—once planted, simply enjoy the perfume and wonderful fall foliage. A quick tip: be sure to buy the plant on its own root stock so it doesn't sucker, because it can revert back to the species. There are numerous crosses of Koreanspice viburnum with other species that are also fabulous for the garden, including Judd viburnum (*Viburnum × juddii*) and Burkwood viburnum (*Viburnum × burkwoodii*).

Height: 2½'–4' (0.8–1.2 m)
Width: 2½'–4' (0.8–1.2 m)
Cold Tolerance: -20°F (-29°C)
Seasons of Interest: Spring–Fall
Lighting Requirements: Full Sun–Part Shade

Korean rhododendron (*Rhododendron mucronulatum*)

This happens to be one of only a few true rhododendrons that are deciduous. Its fall foliage is brilliant in shades of yellow, orange, and rose. One of the earliest of spring bloomers, the beautiful orchid flowers appear before the leaves. Korean rhododendron is ideal situated in a woodland, along an entryway, or in the border. Like all other plants in the heath family (Ericaceae), it does best in acidic soils. The gray bark is attractive in winter with its twisted branches and silvery glow. 'Cornell Pink', 'Album' (white flowers), 'Crater's Edge' (a dwarf 3 feet [0.9 m] tall), and 'Nana' are additional cultivars that give varying color and size choices. Korean rhododendron was brought to the United States in 1882. (See additional information under The Rhododendron Society on page 213.)

Height: 4'–8' (1.2–2.4 m)
Width: 4'–8' (1.2–2.4 m)
Cold Tolerance: -20°F (-29.9°C)
Seasons of Interest: Spring–Fall
Lighting Requirements: Full Sun–Part Shade

Summer Sensations

While roses are a summer staple of the garden, there are lots of other shrubs with great summer interest.

Virginia rose (*Rosa virginiana*)

Native roses are rarely talked about, but here is one of the many native roses that can take its rightful place in our gardens. With deep-green leaves that turn a beautiful orange-red in the fall, Virginia rose can be planted on hillsides to reduce mowing or can be planted in a sunny border garden. It's drought tolerant. Also salt tolerant, the rose can be planted into a low hedge along a busy roadway to create a natural barrier

A Special Small Garden

In a small garden in Germantown, a section of Philadelphia, there sits the oldest rose garden in the country. Wyck Historic House, Garden, and Farm is the place to visit to see old roses. Wyck has been the inspiration for many of our new varieties of roses today. If you want to see the collection at Wyck, visit when the roses are in full bloom because of the amazing fragrances. Not all the roses rebloom. Reblooming roses as we know them today were bred from these early old or antique roses found at Wyck. The transition from old roses to modern roses occurred in 1867 with the development of the first hybrid tea rose, 'La France'. From that time forward, rose breeders of the late nineteenth and early twentieth centuries bred hybrid tea roses for the masses, and in the late twentieth and early twenty-first centuries, the first shrub roses were developed for easy care. Some rose breeders work their entire lives developing roses that are reblooming and disease resistant. When they finally find the perfect roses for the market, after years of evaluation, it can be a once-in-a-lifetime opportunity for them. As consumers, gardeners, and professionals, we shouldn't take for granted what's available to us today—it has literally taken lifetimes to get to us.

In any garden, roses (*Rosa* sp.) are always a welcome sight. Now more than ever the reblooming roses that are on the market can provide bloom from late spring until frost. They come in all forms, including creepers, shrubs, and climbers. The branded lines of roses that have appeared since the turn of the twenty-first century continue to improve in their performance and disease resistance. Because there are so many great roses out there, I couldn't pick just one. On page 64, you will find a list of some of the rose lines, as well as the rose companies that have their selections online to view. Each of us has our own preferences for color, fragrance, and shape of a rose. Go to your local garden center and take your time looking through the myriad of plants. You will find the perfect one for you and make it your own.

List of Rose Brands and Rose Companies

ROSE LINES
Bloomin' Easy® Roses
Drift® Roses
Easy Elegance® Roses
Flower Carpet® Roses or
  The Carpet Rose®
Knock Out® Roses
Meidland® Roses
Oso Easy® Roses
Sunblaze® Miniature Roses
Weeks Roses

ROSE COMPANIES
David Austin® Roses
Heirloom Roses
Jackson & Perkins™ Roses
Star Roses®
Weeks Roses

with its hooked prickles. The single, five-petal pink flowers have a wonderful fragrance and yield bright red hips (fruit) later in the year. Blooms appear in late spring or early summer and it typically does not rebloom. Mrs. Grieve's *A Modern Herbal* talks about the medicinal qualities of the old species roses and their importance in yielding vitamin C when using the hips for tea or to make rose jelly—a sweet treat.

Height: 4'–6' (1.2–1.8 m)
Width: 4'–6' (1.2–1.8 m)
Cold Tolerance: -30°F (-34°C)
Seasons of Interest: Spring–Fall
Lighting Requirements: Full Sun

Seven-son flower (*Heptacodium miconioides*)

Seven-son flower is a shrub that was underappreciated for almost seventy years before nurseries started to carry it. It was brought to the United States from China in 1907 by E. H. Wilson—a plant hunter who changed the American landscape with the plants he discovered in Asia and brought back to the United States—but it never caught on with the nursery trade. Seven-son flower was finally reintroduced to the public in 1980. Since then, it's become quite popular. The performance of seven-son flower in colder regions of the country helps bring diversity and beauty to gardens. *Hepta* means seven and *codium* is a form of seaweed that has dichotomous branching (branching in two), which is how this plant branches—it produces two branches, opposite of each other, along the stem. The seven-son flower gets its common name from the number of blooms that make up each flower cluster. Six flower buds are positioned in a circle around a seventh central bud.

Below: Seven-son flower. Sepals in crimson pink appear after the blooms fade

> **Height:** 20'–25' (6–7.6 m)
> **Width:** 12' (3.6 m)
> **Cold Tolerance:** -30°F (-34°C)
> **Seasons of Interest:** All Seasons
> **Lighting Requirements:** Full Sun–Part Shade

Hydrangea (*Hydrangea* spp.)

Hydrangeas used to be called your grandmother's plant—but not anymore! Since the beginning of the twenty-first century, hydrangeas have been reinvented to give sturdier blooms, more blooms, and the ability to rebloom. They have been bred to be smaller for the city garden and for containers, and to produce larger flowerheads. The flower colors have changed too! And it looks like the momentum is not going to die down anytime soon. When Dr. Michael Dirr helped Bailey Nursery bring the first reblooming mophead hydrangea ENDLESS SUMMER™ The Original (*Hydrangea macrophylla* 'Bailmer') to market in 2004, he noted that it was the first reblooming (remontant) hydrangea of its kind. Newer versions are getting stronger disease resistance, better blooms, and more colorful stems and flowers.

The mophead hydrangeas are not the only hydrangeas either. In making a selection for this chapter, it was difficult to choose one or two hydrangeas to include. You will find a detailed chart on pages 66 to 69 that was put together with the help of growers, but these are not all the hydrangeas on the market. One highlight of the chart lists whether or not the plant reblooms, which is invaluable to know when pruning.

Hydrangea

Bigleaf–*H. macrophylla*	TEMPERATURE	HEIGHT	WIDTH	SEASONS–INTEREST
Abracadabra® 'HorOrb'	-10°F / -23°C°	3'–4' (0.9–1.2 m)	3'–4' (0.9–1.2 m)	Summer–Fall
Abracadabra® 'HorAbstra'	-10°F / -23°C	3'–4' (0.9–1.2 m)	3'–4' (0.9–1.2 m)	Summer–Fall
Bloomin' Easy® Tilt-A-Swirl® 'QUFI'	-10°F / -23°C	3'–4' (0.9–1.2 m)	3'–4' (0.9–1.2 m)	Late Spring–Fall
Cherry Explosion™ 'McKay'	-10°F / -23°C	3' (0.9 m)	3' (0.9 m)	Summer–Fall
Cityline® Berlin 'Berlin Rabe'	-10°F / -23°C	1'–3' (30–90 cm)	1'–3' (30–90 cm)	Summer–Fall
Cityline® Mars 'Ramars'	-10°F / -23°C	2'–3' (61–90 cm)	2'–3' (61–90 cm)	Summer–Fall
Cityline® Paris 'Paris Rapa'	-10°F / -23°C	1'–2' (30–61 cm)	1'–2' (30–61 cm)	Summer–Fall
Cityline® Rio 'Ragra'	-10°F / -23°C	2'–3' (61–90 cm)	2'–3' (61–90 cm)	Summer–Fall
Cityline® Venice 'Venice Raven'	-10°F / -23°C	1'–3' (30–90 cm)	1'–3' (30–90 cm)	Summer–Fall
Cityline® Vienna 'Vienna Rawi'	-10°F / -23°C	1'–3' (30–90 cm)	1'–3' (30–90 cm)	Summer–Fall
Edgy® Hearts 'Horheart'	-10°F / -23°C	2'–4' (0.6–1.2 m)	2'–4' (0.6–1.2 m)	Summer–Fall
Endless Summer® 'Bailmer'	20°F / 29°C	3' 4' (0.9 1.2 m)	4' 5' (1.2 1.5 m)	Late Spring–Fall
Endless Summer® BloomStruck® 'PIIHM-II'	-20°F / -29°C	3'–4' (0.9–1.2 m)	4'–5' (1.2–1.5 m)	Late Spring–Fall
Endless Summer® BlushingBride 'Blushing Bride'	-10°F / -23°C	3'–6' (0.9–1.8 m)	3'–6' (0.9–1.8 m)	Late Spring–Fall
Endless Summer® Summer Crush® 'BAILMACFIVE'	-20°F / -29°C	1.5'–3' (46–90 cm)	1.5'–3' (46–90 cm)	Summer–Fall
Endless Summer® Twist-n-Shout® 'PIIHM-I'	-20°F / -29°C	3'–5' (0.9–1.5 m)	3'–5' (0.9–1.5 m)	Late Spring–Fall
Everlasting® Amethyst 'Hokomathyst'	-10°F / -23°C	2'–2.5' (61–76 cm)	2'–2.5' (61–76 cm)	Late Spring–Fall
Everlasting® Bride 'Hortmabrid'	-10°F / -23°C	2'–2.5' (61–76 cm)	2'–2.5' (61–76 cm)	Late Spring–Fall
Everlasting® Coral 'Hokmac'	-10°F / -23°C	2'–2.5' (61–76 cm)	2'–2.5' (61–76 cm)	Late Spring–Fall
Everlasting® Crimson 'HORTMAGICRI'	-10°F / -23°C	3' (0.9 m)	3' (0.9 m)	Spring–Summer
Everlasting® Garnet 'Kolmgarip'	-10°F / -23°C	2.5'–3' (76–90 cm)	2.5'–3' (76–90 cm)	Summer–Fall
Everlasting® Green Cloud 'Hortmagreclo'	-10°F / -23°C	3'–4' (0.9–1.2 m)	3'–4' (0.9–1.2 m)	Summer–Fall
Everlasting® Harmony 'Hortmahar'	-10°F / -23°C	3'–4' (0.9–1.2 m)	3'–4' (0.9–1.2 m)	Summer–Fall
Everlasting® Jade 'Hortmaja'	-10°F / -23°C	2.5'–3' (76–90 cm)	2.5'–3' (76–90 cm)	Late Spring–Fall
Everlasting® Noblesse 'Hokomano'	-10°F / -23°C	2'–3' (61–90 cm)	2'–3' (61–90 cm)	Late Spring–Fall
Everlasting® Ocean 'Hortmac'	-10°F / -23°C	3'–4' (0.9–1.2 m)	3'–4' (0.9–1.2 m)	Summer–Fall
Everlasting® Opal 'Xian'	-20°F / -29°C	3'–4' (0.9–1.2 m)	3'–4' (0.9–1.2 m)	Summer–Fall
Everlasting® Revolution 'Hokomarero'	-10°F / -23°C	1'–2' (30–61 cm)	1'–2' (30–61 cm)	Summer–Fall

LIGHTING	COLOR(S)	BLOOM TYPE	REBLOOMING
Full Sun–Partial Shade	Green to Peach to Hot Pink	Mophead or Hortensia	No
Full Sun–Partial Shade	Pink	Lacecap	No
Partial Shade	Multicolor, Pink	Mophead or Hortensia	Yes
Full Sun–Partial Shade	Cherry Red	Lacecap	No
Full Sun–Partial Shade	Pink or Blue	Mophead or Hortensia	No
Full Sun–Partial Shade	White with Blue or Pink	Mophead or Hortensia	No
Full Sun–Partial Shade	Red	Mophead or Hortensia	No
Full Sun–Partial Shade	Pink or Blue	Mophead or Hortensia	No
Full Sun–Partial Shade	Pink or Blue	Mophead or Hortensia	No
Full Sun–Partial Shade	Pink or Blue	Mophead or Hortensia	No
Full Sun–Partial Shade	Pink	Mophead or Hortensia	No
Partial Shade	Pink, Purple or Blue	Mophead or Hortensia	Yes
Partial Shade	Rose-Pink or Purple	Mophead or Hortensia	Yes
Partial Shade	Blush Pink or Blue	Mophead or Hortensia	Yes
Full Sun–Partial Shade	Raspberry Red or Neon Purple	Mophead or Hortensia	Yes
Partial Shade	Deep Pink or Periwinkle Blue	Lacecap	Yes
Full Sun–Partial Shade	Fuchsia Pink or Violet Blue	Mophead or Hortensia	Yes
Full Sun–Partial Shade	White	Mophead or Hortensia	Yes
Full Sun–Partial Shade	Coral to Blue	Mophead or Hortensia	Yes
Full Sun–Partial Shade	Green to Red	Mophead or Hortensia	Yes
Full Sun–Partial Shade	Bright Pink with Blue edge or Lime Green with Pink edge	Mophead or Hortensia	Yes
Full Sun–Partial Shade	Green to Red	Mophead or Hortensia	Yes
Full Sun–Partial Shade	Soft Pink with Blue Eye	Mophead or Hortensia	Yes
Full Sun–Partial Shade	Apple to White to Green	Mophead or Hortensia	Yes
Full Sun–Partial Shade	White to Green	Mophead or Hortensia	Yes
Full Sun–Partial Shade	Baby Pink	Mophead or Hortensia	Yes
Full Sun–Partial Shade	Pink	Mophead or Hortensia	Yes
Full Sun–Partial Shade	Deep Pink to Maroon to Blue	Mophead or Hortensia	No

	TEMPERATURE	HEIGHT	WIDTH	SEASONS–INTEREST
Felcity 'Tomeina-blue'	0°F / -18°C	4'–5' (1.2–1.5 m)	4'–5' (1.2–1.5 m)	Summer–Fall
Hovaria™ 'Hobella'	0°F / -18°C	3'–5' (0.9–1.5 m)	3'–5' (0.9–1.5 m)	Summer–Fall
L.A. Dreamin'® 'Lindsey Ann'	-10°F / -23°C	4' (1.2 m)	4' (1.2 m)	Summer–Fall
Let's Dance® Big Easy® 'Berner'	-10°F / -23°C	2'–3' (61–90 cm)	2'–3' (61–90 cm)	Summer–Fall
Let's Dance® Blue Jangles® 'SMHMTAU'	-10°F / -23°C	1'–2' (30–61 cm)	1'–2' (30–61 cm)	Summer–Fall
Let's Dance Diva!™ 'SMHMLDD'	-10°F / -23°C	3'–4' (0.9–1.2 m)	3'–4' (0.9–1.2 m)	Summer–Fall
Let's Dance® Rave™ 'SMNHMSIGMA'	-10°F / -23°C	2'–3' (61–90 cm)	2'–3' (61–90 cm)	Summer–Fall
Let's Dance® Rhythmic Blue® 'SMHMES14'	-10°F / -23°C	3'–4' (0.9–1.2 m)	3'–4' (0.9–1.2 m)	Summer–Fall
Let's Dance® Starlight 'Lynn'	-10°F / -23°C	2'–3' (61–90 cm)	2'–3' (61–90 cm)	Summer–Fall
'Nikko Blue'	-10°F / -23°C	4'–6' (1.2–1.8 m)	4'–6' (1.2–1.8 m)	Summer–Fall
Paraplu® 'SMHMP1'	-10°F / -23°C	3'–3' (0.9–0.9 m)	3'–3' (0.9–0.9 m)	Summer–Fall

Bracted–*H. involucrata*	TEMPERATURE	HEIGHT	WIDTH	SEASONS–INTEREST
Blue Bunny™ 'Wim Rutten'	0°F / -18°C	2'–4' (0.6–1.2 m)	2'–4' (0.6–1.2 m)	Late Summer–Fall

Mountain–*H. serrata*	TEMPERATURE	HEIGHT	WIDTH	SEASONS–INTEREST
'Blue Billow'	0°F / -18°C	4'–5' (1.2–1.5 m)	4'–5' (1.2–1.5 m)	Summer–Fall
'Bluebird'	-10°F / -23°C	4' (1.2 m)	4' (1.2 m)	Summer–Fall
Tiny Tuff Stuff™ 'MAKD'	-10°F / -23°C	1.5'–2' (46–61 cm)	1.5'–2' (46–61 cm)	Summer–Fall
Tuff Stuff™ 'MAK20'	-10°F / -23°C	2'–3' (61–90 cm)	2'–3' (61–90 cm)	Summer–Fall
Tuff Stuff Ah-Ha® 'SMNHSDD'	-10°F / -23°C	2'–3' (61–90 cm)	2'–3' (61–90 cm)	Summer–Fall
Tuff Stuff™–Red 'SMNMAKTSR'	-10°F / -23°C	2'–3' (61–90 cm)	2'–3' (61–90 cm)	Summer–Fall

Oakleaf–*H. quercifolia*	TEMPERATURE	HEIGHT	WIDTH	SEASONS–INTEREST
Gatsby Gal™ 'Brenhill'	-10°F / -23°C	5'–6' (1.5–1.8 m)	5'–6' (1.5–1.8 m)	Summer–Winter
Gatsby Moon™ 'Brother Edward'	-10°F / -23°C	6'–8' (1.8–2.4 m)	6'–8' (1.8–2.4 m)	Summer–Winter
Gatsby Pink® 'JoAnn'	-10°F / -23°C	6'–8' (1.8–2.4 m)	6'–8' (1.8–2.4 m)	Summer–Winter
Gatsby Star™ 'Doughill'	-10°F / -23°C	6'–8' (1.8–2.4 m)	6'–8' (1.8–2.4 m)	Summer–Winter
'Munchkin'	-10°F / -23°C	3'–4.5' (0.9–1.4 m)	3'–4.5' (0.9–1.4 m)	Summer–Winter

LIGHTING	COLOR(S)	BLOOM TYPE	REBLOOMING
Full Sun–Partial Shade	Pink	Modified Lacecap	No
Full Sun–Partial Shade	Light Pink to Lime Green to Deep Cherry Red	Lacecap	No
Full Sun–Partial Shade	Pink to Purple to Blue	Mophead or Hortensia	Partial
Full Sun–Partial Shade	Pink or Lavender	Mophead or Hortensia	Yes
Full Sun–Partial Shade	Pink or Blue	Mophead or Hortensia	Yes
Full Sun–Partial Shade	Pink or Lavender	Lacecap	Yes
Full Sun–Partial Shade	Bright Pink or Purple	Mophead or Hortensia	Yes
Full Sun–Partial Shade	Pink or Blue	Mophead or Hortensia	Yes
Full Sun–Partial Shade	Pink or Lavender	Lacecap	Yes
Partial Shade	Dutch Blue; can have touches of pink	Mophead or Hortensia	No
Full Sun–Partial Shade	Pink or Purple	Mophead or Hortensia	No

LIGHTING	COLOR(S)	BLOOM TYPE	REBLOOMING
Full Sun–Partial Shade	White, Blue	Lacecap	No

LIGHTING	COLOR(S)	BLOOM TYPE	REBLOOMING
Full Sun–Partial Shade	Blue	Lacecap	Yes
Full Sun–Partial Shade	Blue	Lacecap	Yes
Full Sun–Partial Shade	Light Pink or Blue	Lacecap	Yes
Full Sun–Partial Shade	Pink or Purple	Lacecap	Yes
Full Sun–Partial Shade	Pink or Blue	Lacecap	Yes
Full Sun–Partial Shade	Red	Lacecap	Yes

LIGHTING	COLOR(S)	BLOOM TYPE	REBLOOMING
Full Sun–Partial Shade	White	Lacecap	No
Full Sun–Partial Shade	White	Lacecap	No
Full Sun–Partial Shade	White changing to Pink	Lacecap	No
Full Sun Partial Shade	White	Lacecap	No
Partial Shade	Pink	Lacecap	No

Panicle–*H. paniculata*	TEMPERATURE	HEIGHT	WIDTH	SEASONS–INTEREST
Bloomin' Easy® Candelabra® 'Hpopr013'	-30°F / -34°C	4'–6' (1.2–1.8 m)	4'–6' (1.2–1.8 m)	Summer–Winter
Bloomin' Easy® Flare™ 'Kolmavesu'	-30°F / -34°C	2'–3' (61–90 cm)	2'–3' (61–90 cm)	Summer–Winter
Bloomin' Easy® Moonrock™ 'Kolmakilima'	-30°F / -34°C	4'–6' (1.2–1.8 m)	4'–6' (1.2–1.8 m)	Summer–Winter
Bobo® 'ILVOBO'	-30°F / -34°C	2.5'–3' (76–90 cm)	2.5'–3' (76–90 cm)	Summer–Winter
Fire Light® 'SMHPFL'	-30°F / -34°C	6'–8' (1.8–2.4 m)	6'–8' (1.8–2.4 m)	Summer–Winter
'Limelight'	-30°F / -34°C	6'–8' (1.8–2.4 m)	6'–8' (1.8–2.4 m)	Summer–Winter
'Little Lamb'	-30°F / -34°C	4'–6' (1.2–1.8 m)	4'–6' (1.2–1.8 m)	Summer–Winter
Little Lime® 'Jane'	-30°F / -34°C	3'–5' (0.9–1.5 m)	3'–5' (0.9–1.5 m)	Summer–Winter
Little Quick Fire® 'SMHPLQF'	-30°F / -34°C	3'–5' (0.9–1.5 m)	3'–5' (0.9–1.5 m)	Summer–Winter
Pinky Winky® 'DVPpinky'	-30°F / -34°C	6'–8' (1.8–2.4 m)	6'–8' (1.8–2.4 m)	Summer–Winter
Quick Fire® 'Bulk'	-30°F / -34°C	6'–8' (1.8–2.4 m)	6'–8' (1.8–2.4 m)	Summer–Winter
ZinfinDoll™ 'SMNHPRZEP'	-30°F / -34°C	4'–6' (1.2–1.8 m)	4'–6' (1.2–1.8 m)	Summer–Winter
Vanilla Strawberry™ 'Rehny'	-20°F / -29°C	6'–7' (1.8–2.1 m)	4'–5' (1.2–1.5 m)	Summer–Winter

Rough-leaved–*H. aspera*	TEMPERATURE	HEIGHT	WIDTH	SEASONS–INTEREST
Plum Passion®	-10°F / -23°C	5'–6' (1.5–1.8 m)	5'–6' (1.5–1.8 m)	Summer–Fall

Smooth–*H. arborescens*	TEMPERATURE	HEIGHT	WIDTH	SEASONS–INTEREST
'Haas' Halo'	-30°F / -34°C	3'–5' (0.9–1.5 m)	3'–5' (0.9–1.5 m)	Summer–Fall
Incrediball® 'Abetwo'	-30°F / -34°C	4'–5' (1.2–1.5 m)	4'–5' (1.2–1.5 m)	Summer–Fall
Incrediball® Blush 'NCHA4'	-30°F / -34°C	4'–5' (1.2–1.5 m)	4'–5' (1.2–1.5 m)	Summer–Fall
Invincibelle Limetta™ 'NCHA8'	-30°F / -34°C	3'–4' (0.9–1.2 m)	3'–4' (0.9–1.2 m)	Summer–Fall
Invincibelle Mini Mauvette™ 'NCHA7'	-30°F / -34°C	2.5'–3' (76–90 cm)	2.5'–3' (76–90 cm)	Summer–Fall
Invincibelle® Ruby 'NCHA3'	-30°F / -34°C	3'–4' (0.9–1.2 m)	3'–4' (0.9–1.2 m)	Summer–Fall
Invincibelle® Spirit II 'NCHA2'	-30°F / -34°C	3.5'–4' (1–1.2 m)	3.5'–4' (1–1.2 m)	Summer–Fall
Invincibelle Wee White® 'NCHA5'	-30°F / -34°C	1'–2.5' (30–76 cm)	1'–2.5' (30–76 cm)	Summer–Fall
Rickey® 'SMNHALR'	-30°F / -34°C	4'–5' (1.2–1.5 m)	4'–5' (1.2–1.5 m)	Summer–Fall

Smooth or Silver Leaf—*H. arborescens* ssp. *radiata*	TEMPERATURE	HEIGHT	WIDTH	SEASONS–INTEREST
'Samantha'	-30°F / -34°C	10' (3 m)	10' (3 m)	Summer–Fall

LIGHTING	COLOR(S)	BLOOM TYPE	REBLOOMING
Full Sun–Partial Shade	Multicolor, White	Panicle	No
Full Sun–Partial Shade	Multicolor, White	Panicle	No
Full Sun–Partial Shade	Multicolor, White	Panicle	No
Full Sun–Partial Shade	White changing to Pink	Panicle	No
Full Sun–Partial Shade	White changing to Red	Mophead or Hortensia	No
Full Sun–Partial Shade	Green changing to Burgundy	Mophead or Hortensia	No
Full Sun–Partial Shade	White changing to Pale Pink	Mophead or Hortensia	No
Full Sun–Partial Shade	Green changing to Burgundy	Mophead or Hortensia	No
Full Sun–Partial Shade	White changing to Red	Lacecap	No
Full Sun–Partial Shade	White changing to Pink	Lacecap	No
Full Sun–Partial Shade	White changing to Red	Lacecap	No
Full Sun–Partial Shade	White changing to Red and Pink	Mophead or Hortensia	No
Full Sun–Partial Shade	White to Pink to Rose	Panicle	No

LIGHTING	COLOR(S)	BLOOM TYPE	REBLOOMING
Full Shade–Partial Shade	White with Plum foliage	Lacecap	No

LIGHTING	COLOR(S)	BLOOM TYPE	REBLOOMING
Full Sun–Partial Shade	White–Green	Lacecap	No
Full Sun–Partial Shade	White	Mophead or Hortensia	No
Full Sun–Partial Shade	Pink	Mophead or Hortensia	Yes
Full Sun–Partial Shade	Green	Mophead or Hortensia	Yes
Full Sun–Partial Shade	Mauve-Pink	Mophead or Hortensia	Yes
Full Sun–Partial Shade	Red-Pink	Mophead or Hortensia	Yes
Full Sun–Partial Shade	Pink	Mophead or Hortensia	Yes
Full Sun–Partial Shade	White	Mophead or Hortensia	Yes
Full Sun–Partial Shade	Green with Pink pollen	Mophead or Hortensia	No

LIGHTING	COLOR(S)	BLOOM TYPE	REBLOOMING
Partial Shade	Pinkish-White	Mophead or Hortensia	No

Japanese orixa (*Orixa japonica* 'Pearl Frost')

This lovely shrub has a reputation for being a bit rare in the trade, but it is well worth seeking out. 'Pearl Frost' is a variegated variation of the species and has the adaptability to grow in full sun, but it glows in shade. Fall color is pale yellow.

Height: 10' (3 m)
Width: 10' (3 m)
Cold Tolerance: -10°F (-23°C)
Seasons of Interest: Summer
Lighting Requirements: Full Sun–Part Shade

Top: Japanese orixa

Bottom: Tea viburnum with its red berries and long colorful drooping leaves

Fall Fashion

With fall comes the amazing burst of brilliant colors before our world falls into its deep sleep. Plants take on a new character as the sky becomes clearer and cooler. The shorter days and cooler nighttime temperatures begin the process of senescence in the plants. As the chlorophyll begins to withdraw from leaves, other plant pigments, such as anthocyanins and carotenoids, become more vivid. The color changes in leaves and brings on an entirely new look to the garden. Colored leaves and berries also play a vital role for animals looking for food sources. In the case of birds, berried plants offer fruits that are high in fat and protein for their long migratory travels. (See Chapter 9 for more information on attracting wildlife.)

Tea viburnum (*Viburnum setigerum*)

The bowing branches of the tea viburnum, laden with candied-apple-red berries in the fall, entice birds to feast as they migrate south or as they prepare for the coming winter. The fall foliage of this shrub is an amazing pink, red, burgundy, or orange color. Tea viburnum was first introduced into the United States in 1901 from China by E. H. Wilson. You can make tea from the leaves of this plant, which gives it its common name. The species name means "bristle" due to the structure of the leaf veins ending with a bristle. The flower cymes (flat or slightly domed collections of small flowers) are not very showy in larger landscapes, but in more intimate locations, the blooms add to the ambiance. The plant's overall stature is upright and vase shaped, with bare stems beneath. The shrub lends itself well to mass plantings

Blackhaw viburnum

against a green, cream, or white backdrop for its fall display. Under-plant the shrub with spring bulbs and woodland poppies, followed by summer-flowering perennials, to add interest to the landscape while the shrub is readying for its fall show. Full sun yields the best display of berries and foliage. There is an orange-berried form introduced by Wilson in 1907; it goes by the name 'Aurantiacum'.

Height: 8'–12' (2.4–3.6 m)
Width: 6'–8' (1.8–2.4 m)
Cold Tolerance: -20°F (-28.4°C)
Seasons of Interest: Spring–Fall
Lighting Requirements: Full Sun–Part Shade

Blackhaw viburnum (*Viburnum prunifolium*)

This small tree or large shrub grows in a range of environments, including underneath black walnut (*Juglans nigra*) trees. Its opposite simple leaves are green all season until they turn a barn-red to plum in the fall. The cymes of flowers in the spring have an aminoid smell, later yielding rose-pink fruits that turn a deep blue-black and taste like prunes. You can make jams and jellies from the fruits. Overall the plant is more upright in form, ideal for hedging, borders, woodlands, or as a small tree. Ideal if you like to watch birds and other wildlife. It's one of our North American natives.

Height: 12'–15' (3.6–4.5 m)
Width: 6'–12' (1.8–3.6 m)
Cold Tolerance: -30°F (-34°C)
Seasons of Interest: Spring Fall
Lighting Requirements: Full Sun–Part Shade

Purple beautyberry (*Callicarpa dichotoma*)

The deep rich jewel-toned purple of this shrub's berries adds an amazing dimension to the fall garden. If you are a flower arranger, the long branches of berries hold up well in arrangements, especially if designed in a pumpkin. Their new growth bears the flowers and the fruit, and you can prune this shrub to the ground to rejuvenate when necessary. It arrived on the shores of the United States in 1857 from Japan and has worked its way into the hearts of many gardeners. There is even a variegated form with white berries called 'Duet' that is equally striking in the fall. American beautyberry (*Callicarpa americana*) is a larger shrub with larger berries used by Native Americans for medicinal purposes. This is another beautiful shrub.

Height: 2'–4' (0.6–1.2 m)
Width: 3'–5' (0.9–1.5 m)
Cold Tolerance: -10°F (-23°C)
Seasons of Interest: Spring–Fall
Lighting Requirements: Full Sun–Part Shade

Below: Purple beautyberry

Right: Eastern wahoo

Eastern wahoo or spindle tree (*Euonymus atropurpureus*)

This unique shrub was used to make spindles for spinning thread. It was also used to make spindles on chairs, as the wood is tough and can withstand heavy weight. Planted in the woods, along a woodland edge, or in full sun as a specimen, the large shrub will not disappoint. The carmine-colored blooms in June yield a four-sided fruit in the fall that splits open, revealing the seed inside. Ideal for attracting wild-life. This shrub is still underutilized.

Height: 12'–20' (3.6–6 m)
Width: 15'–25' (4.5–7.6 m)
Cold Tolerance: -10°F (-23°C)
Seasons of Interest: Spring–Fall
Lighting Requirements: Full Sun–Part Shade

Winter Stature, Shape, Form, and Line

For many people, winter is the time to retreat into the house and be less active. Plants also retreat in the winter to conserve their energy, restore damaged roots, and store more energy and food for their flower and leaf buds. Some may change bark color, which makes their surfaces more interesting to view. Plants that have interesting bark and form are best placed where they can be seen as you pass by the front or back doors. Here are some plants that have great winter interest for your enjoyment.

Paperbush or edgeworthia (*Edgeworthia chrysantha*)

Once relegated to botanic gardens and private collectors' gardens, this shrub is finally making its way to consumers. The large 3- to 5½-inch (7 to 14 cm) leaves make this plant look tropical, especially in more northern locations. The stems are beautiful to look at in the winter, particularly the leaf scars. And in late winter the shrub begins to bloom with a sweet fragrant essence. The flower buds look like little silk mittens protecting the downward-facing tubular flowers from freezing. Once the flowers are open, the leaves begin to emerge, standing straight up like feathers. Plant paperbush near a walkway in a protected spot to enjoy the late-winter blooms in February through April, depending on the winter temperatures. The plant was introduced to the United States from China in 1845 and was used for making high-quality paper. When the plant is young the stems can be tied in knots.

Height: 4'–6' (1.2–1.8 m)
Width: 4'–6' (1.2–1.8 m)
Cold Tolerance: 10°F (-23°C)
Seasons of Interest: All Seasons
Lighting Requirements: Part Shade

Top: Toothache tree fruit

Middle: Toothache tree bark

Bottom: Harry Lauder's walking stick

Toothache tree or prickly ash (*Zanthoxylum americanum*)

Large spines up and down the trunk of this plant make it look like something out of *Jurassic Park*. The Native Americans used the fruit and bark to numb their mouths when they had tooth problems. The small fruits are spicy and numbing and can be used in Sichuan cooking (there is an Asian form of this tree as well). Native from Quebec to Virginia, it's a conversation starter in any garden. Ideal for making hedgerows or loose borders, toothache tree does well in poor dry soils and can be planted in full sun or shade. If you're an animal lover, this tree is a must-have, as it attracts birds like bobwhites, pheasants, and quail, and giant swallowtail butterflies lay their eggs on the leaves. The fall color is a muted yellow to green like the flowers in the spring, which emit a citrusy fragrance. The berries have an interesting pink to deep rose-colored covering with shiny black seeds inside. There is a Southern version of the plant called southern prickly-ash (*Zanthoxylum clava-herculis*) and an Asian version called Chinese pepper (*Zanthoxylum simulans*).

Height: 15'–20' (4.5–6 m)
Width: 10'–15' (3–4.5 m)
Cold Tolerance: -30°F (-34°C)
Seasons of Interest: All Seasons
Lighting Requirements: Full Sun–Part Shade

Harry Lauder's walking stick (*Corylus avellana* 'Contorta')

Also known as European filbert, this specimen shrub has amazing twisted stems that have fascinated people for decades. If you like floral design, the stems are perfect for arranging. Plant near a window or walkway to enjoy the plant in the winter. In the summer the shrub is covered in twisted leaves. Tiny female flowers sit right above the male flower catkins, which are spectacular in the spring. Little maintenance is required.

Height: 8'–10' (2.4–3 m)
Width: 8'–10' (2.4–3 m)
Cold Tolerance: -20°F (-29°C)
Seasons of Interest: All Seasons
Lighting Requirements: Full Sun–Part Shade

Hollies (*Ilex* spp.)

There are many hollies that could be addressed in this section; however, only a few will be mentioned for the sake of brevity. Hollies are dioecious, meaning the male and female flowers are produced on separate plants. This means that for many varieties, in order to get berries, you need to have both male and female shrubs of the same species present.

• **The Chinese holly or Burford holly (*Ilex cornuta* 'Burfordii')** can go it alone or have a male holly for pollination and seed production. It's parthenocarpic, which means it will produce fruit without seed, just like a seedless watermelon. The leaves are lustrous dark green with a single spine at the end of the leaf. And the new growth looks identical to the parent plant, with five spines later turning to one spine with age. The

Burford holly

fruit production on the Burford holly can be ridiculously heavy and gorgeous. Bigger birds with larger beak capacities eat the fruit. There are numerous dwarf cultivars and more to come. One thing to note—if the winter gets exceptionally cold, it may drop leaves. But not to worry; it will come back full force in spring. Because of its lower stature it makes an excellent barrier or focal point, and it is attractive when limbed up as a small tree.

• **The longstalk holly (*Ilex pedunculosa*)** is a spineless holly that has a small simple leaf, and the fruit hangs off a long stalk—hence its common name. Longstalk is great as a focal point for the summer or winter garden. 'Vleck' is the only known cultivar and is rarely found in the marketplace. Keep an eye on this holly for future introductions.

• **Japanese holly (*Ilex crenata*)** has been around quite a while, with many cultivars from small to large. This holly is commonly used in residential landscapes. It wouldn't surprise me if there were many more cultivars waiting in the wings. The leaves are small and spineless.

Other hollies to consider are English holly (*Ilex aquifolium*) and holly Nellie R. Stevens (*Ilex* 'Nellie R. Stevens'), which is a cross between English holly and Chinese holly. Both hollies are great for hedging and in groups. Be sure to have a compatible male if you want berries.

Height: 10'–15' (3–4.5 m)
Width: 8'–10' (2.4–3 m)
Cold Tolerance: 10°F (-23°C)
Seasons of Interest: All Seasons
Lighting Requirements: Full Sun–Part Shade

Above: The eye of the dragon—Japanese black pine

Right: Willowleaf cotoneaster on a winter day

Japanese black pine (*Pinus thunbergii* 'Oculus Draconis')

This shrub has a truly amazing habit of sprawling across the ground in stiff stature like 'Thunderhead'. 'Oculus Draconis' translates to "eye of the dragon." The endearing quality that gave this plant its cultivar name is the yellow bands on the two fascicle bundle needle clusters. The species of 'Oculus Draconis' was brought to the United States in 1855, and the entire group of plants continues to be sold in the marketplace. Japanese black pine has naturalized in parts of New Jersey and Delaware, cross-pollinating with other local pines. The shrub doesn't blink when it comes to salt spray, which is why it does so well along the coastline. The buds are prominent features when they begin to elongate. The cultivar is highly collectible.

Height: 15'–20' (4.5–6 m)
Width: 20'–30' (6–9 m)
Cold Tolerance: 0°F (-18°C)
Seasons of Interest: All Seasons
Lighting Requirements: Full Sun

Willowleaf cotoneaster (*Cotoneaster salicifolius*)

There are over thirty cultivars of this plant, in all sorts of shapes and sizes, including creeping forms. The species is a tall shrub that cascades with an amazing fall display of red berries. The leaves are elongated like a willow leaf. This native from Western China was introduced to the United States in 1908 and made its way into botanic gardens and onto large estates. Flowers are small, white, individual blooms that appear on flat-topped corymbs in May through June. Their fragrance is pungent. It's best planted in full sun and can tolerate shade, but will have fewer flowers and berries. It can also tolerate dry soils. The fall and winter displays eclipse the spring flowering, and the evergreen nature of the plant makes it a wonderful buffer. Birds adore the berries in winter.

Height: 10'–15' (3–4.5 m)
Width: 10'–15' (3–4.5 m)
Cold Tolerance: 0°F (-18°C)
Seasons of Interest: All Seasons
Lighting Requirements: Full Sun–Part Shade

Witch hazel 'Jelena'

Witch hazel (*Hamamelis* spp.)

Witch hazels have never been more popular than they are today. Many botanic gardens have collections of witch hazels on display. I recommend visiting on a bright winter day with pencil, paper, and camera in hand to make note of your favorites based on color, shape, and fragrance. If you don't have a botanic garden or arboretum close by, visit a local garden center to see what they have in inventory. Every garden needs at least one witch hazel. The species and the hybrids are all showy in their own right, and on a sunny winter day, the fragrances attract pollinators from afar before the temperatures drop back down at night. Go to Chapter 6 to see the vernal witch hazel, one specimen that I highly recommend. If you buy any of the hybrids, try to buy them on their own roots, not grafted to a root stock. Graft unions can sometimes be compromised, and suckers will grow. Sprouts from the root stock will take over if you are not diligent in pruning them out. Witch hazel 'Jelena' (*Hamamelis* × *intermedia* 'Jelena') is my top choice. The cross is between the Chinese and Japanese witch hazels. The color of the flower is a coppery orange, and it has long strappy petals that roll open during the day and roll closed at night. The fragrance is mild, and the plant blooms from February through March, creating a warm glow in the garden. The cultivars are tolerant to a wide variety of growing conditions. Once you have one witch hazel, you will want more!

Height: 8'–12' (2.4–3.6 m)
Width: 8'–12' (2.4–3.6 m)
Cold Tolerance: -10°F (-23°C)
Seasons of Interest: All Seasons
Lighting Requirements: Full Sun–Part Shade

CHAPTER 5

TAILORED TO FIT— DESIGNING WITH SHRUBS

Designing home gardens that include shrubs should be fun. The process should address the needs of you and your family. It also should have a practical side to the design, so when the family changes, your garden can change, too. Children's play areas are transformed into quiet areas for teen studies or socializing. Imagine first and build second. Visualize what you want and need and then put the ideas onto paper. See if there is anything missing and make your checklist. Creating the checklist clarifies and solidifies your desires for your garden.

You might want to make some areas of your garden low-maintenance, or perhaps you want to add color for different times of the year. Because not everyone is interested in garden design or has the time or expertise to build landscape plans from scratch, the following three professionally designed planting plans are a great place to start. Use them to build a foundation for designing your own landscape plantings and for incorporating more shrubs into your garden. These designs provide ideas for how to use shrubs to reduce overall maintenance and to provide multi-dimensional interest from the ground level to the treetops.

Winter Interest Shrub Planting

Even though you may not spend as much time out in the garden in the winter months as you do when the weather is warm, you'll want to add plants that stimulate beauty and interest all year round. A walk in the winter garden for just a few moments a day can help restore focus and clarity. This garden is situated outside the dwelling's large picture window so that a majority of the garden can be seen from inside. When winters are cold and bleak, a colorful landscape lifts the spirits.

Opposite: Home with Catawba rhododendron (*Rhododendron catawbiense*)

Right: Late winter blooms of witch hazel 'Premivera' (*Hamamelis* x *intermedia* 'Premivera')

Plants for a Winter Garden

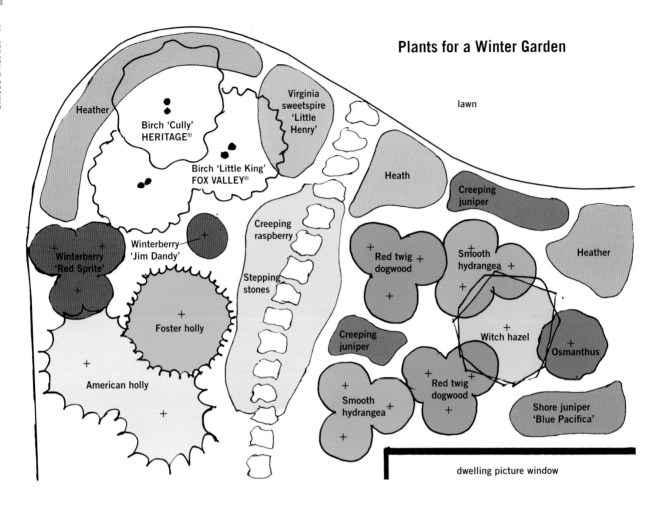

lawn

Heather

Birch 'Cully'
HERITAGE®

Virginia
sweetspire
'Little
Henry'

Heath

Creeping
juniper

Birch 'Little King'
FOX VALLEY®

Heather

Winterberry
'Jim Dandy'

Creeping
raspberry

Red twig
dogwood

Smooth
hydrangea

Winterberry
'Red Sprite'

Stepping
stones

Foster holly

Creeping
juniper

Witch hazel

Osmanthus

American holly

Smooth
hydrangea

Red twig
dogwood

Shore juniper
'Blue Pacifica'

dwelling picture window

River birch—*Betula nigra* 'Cully' HERITAGE®
-20°F 40'–70' × 40'–60'
(-29°C 12.2–21 m × 12.2–18 m)

River birch—*Betula nigra* 'Little King'
FOX VALLEY®
-20°F 8'–10' × 9'–12'
(-29°C 2.4–3 m × 2.7–3.6 m)

Osmanthus or false holly—
Osmanthus heterophyllus 'Goshiki'
0°F 3'–5' × 4'
(-18°C 0.9–1.5 m × 1.2 m)

Oakleaf hydrangea—*Hydrangea quercifolia*
-10°F 6'–8' × 6'–8'
(-23°C 1.8–2.4 m × 1.8–2.4 m)

Foster holly—*Ilex* × *attenuata* 'Longwood Gold'
0°F 20'–30' × 12'–15'
(-18°C 6–9 m × 3.6–4.5 m)

Red twig dogwood—*Cornus sericea*
-30°F 6'–9' × 7'–10'
(-29°C 1.8–2.7 m × 2.1–3 m)

Winterberry—*Ilex verticillata* 'Red Sprite'
-30°F 3'–5' × 3'–5'
(-34°C 0.9–1.5 m × 0.9–1.5 m)

Witch hazel—*Hamamelis* × *intermedia*
'Jelena'
-10°F 8'–12' × 8'–12'
(-23°C 2.4–3.6 m × 2.4–3.6 m)

American holly—*Ilex opaca* 'Maryland Dwarf'
-10°F 2'–3' × 3'–10'
(-23°F 0.6–0.9 m × 0.9–3 m)

Creeping juniper—*Juniperus horizontalis*
'Bar Harbor'
-30°F ¾'–1' × 5'–6'
(-34°C 23–30 cm × 1.5–1.8 m)

Shore juniper—*Juniperus conferta*
'Blue Pacific'
0°F ½'–1' × 4'–6'
(-18°C 15–30 cm × 1.2–1.8 m)

Creeping raspberry—*Rubus pentalobus*
0°F ½' × 10'
(-18°C 15 cm × 3 m)

Heath—*Erica carnea*
-10°F ½'–1' × ½'–1'
(-23°C 15–30 cm × 18–30 cm)

Scotch heather—*Calluna vulgaris*
-20°F 1'–2' × 1'–2'
(-29°C 30–61 cm × 30–61 cm)

Winterberry—*Ilex verticillata* 'Jim Dandy'
-30°F 3'–6' × 3'–6'
(-34°C 0.9–1.8 × 0.9–1.8 m)

Above, left: Shore juniper 'Blue Pacifica'

Above, right: False Holly 'Goshiki'

Below: Witch hazel 'Jelena'

Shore juniper covers the ground immediately outside the window and allows an unobstructed view, directing your eye to the witch hazel and the false holly. To the left side of the window a nice stand of oakleaf hydrangeas hold their leaves in winter in warmer climates. In colder climates they may drop the majority of leaves, but the flower heads are still there to provide interest. The red twig dogwoods pick up the red highlights in the witch hazel when it blooms.

The variegated color in the false holly has pink new growth in spring. The word Goshiki refers to the five colors that are exhibited in the plant's foliage.

When walking in the winter garden the clean smell of witch hazel 'Jelena' awakens the senses.

Above: Oakleaf hydrangea

Right: Red twig dogwood

Below: Horizontal juniper 'Bar Harbor'

Mounds of Scotch heather and heath in large sweeps bloom in lavender and dusty rose. The flowers also attract pollinators in the full sun. The cool blue-green of horizontal juniper looks like a carpet sprawling across the earth.

Berries and blooms make the landscape colorful throughout the winter. The river birch has papery and curly bark. And the birches create a nice progression of height.

The horizontal American hollies next to the tall pyramid Foster holly provides a strong juxtaposition. And the stone path is swimming in evergreen creeping raspberry.

Left: Foster holly
'Longwood Gold', Longwood
Gardens, Kennett Square,
Pennsylvania

Below, left: River birch
HERITAGE®

Below: River birch FOX
VALLEY®, Scott Arboretum,
Swarthmore, Pennsylvania

Edge Planting

The edge design is a special garden that offers extra biodiversity while reducing overall maintenance and runoff. Edge areas attract a greater number of birds and beneficial insects. Edges or ecotones are habitats that soften sound—especially along a busy roadway—and create a plant barrier to a woodland, to a pond area, or to protect more fragile plant communities or plant collections. The edge also helps stabilize temperatures within the insular planting area, creating mini microclimates.

Plants for the Edge Garden

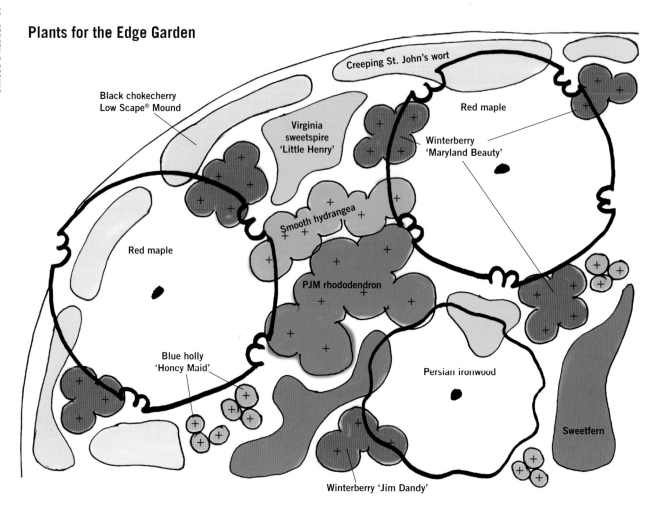

Red maple—*Acer rubrum*
-30°F 40'–70' × 30'–50'
(-34°C 12.2– 21.3 m × 9–15.2 m)

Persian ironwood—*Parrotia persica*
-20°F 20'–40' × 20'–30'
(-29° 6.1–12.2 m × 6.1–9 m)

PJM rhododendron—*Rhododendron*
(PJM Group)
-20°F 3'–6' × 3'–7'
(-29° 0.9–1.8 m × 0.9–2.1 m)

Winterberry—*Ilex verticillata*
'Maryland Beauty'
-20°F 5'–7' × 5'–7'
(-29° 1.5–2.1 m × 1.5–2.1 m)

Winterberry—*Ilex verticillata* 'Jim Dandy'
-30°F 3'–6' × 4'–8'
(-34° 0.9–1.8 m × 1.2–2.4 m)

Blue holly—*Ilex × meserveae* 'Honey Maid'
0°F 3' × 3'
(-18°C 0.9 m × 0.9 m)

Creeping St. John's wort—*Hypericum calycinum*
-10°F 5'–7' × 5'–7'
(-23°C 1.5–2.1 m × 1.5–2.1 m)

Black chokeberry—*Aronia melanocarpa*
'UCONNAM165' Low Scape® Mound
-30°F 1'–2' × 2'–3'
(-34° 30–61 cm × 61–90 cm)

Sweet fern—*Comptonia peregrina*
-40°F 2'–5' × 4'–8'
(-40°C 0.6–1.5 m × 1.2–2.4 m)

Smooth hydrangea—*Hydrangea arborescens*
'NCHA8' INVINCIBELLE LIMETTA®
-30°F 3'–4' × 3'–4'
(-34°C 0.9–1.2 m × 0.9–1.2 m)

Virginia sweetspire—*Itea virginica* 'Sprich'
LITTLE HENRY®
-10°F 1 ½'–2' × 2'–2½'
(-23° 46–61 cm × 61–76 cm)

Red maples are wonderful, slow-growing trees. They produce a plethora of seed in the spring for birds returning from their winter habitats. The Persian ironwood provides a red late-winter glow and a feeding opportunity for pollinators. The fall color of both trees is spectacular. The PJM rhododendron not only provides orchid blooms in spring but also stays evergreen all year long. Its foliage changes color from bright green to deep burgundy as the temperatures get colder.

The black chokeberry cultivar is a newer plant on the market that is a carpet of spring bloom and has berries later in the year for birds or humans (yes, they're edible!).

Red maple, Ambler Arboretum, Ambler, Pennsylvania

Opposite: Winterberry 'Maryland Beauty'

Right: PJM Rhododendron

Far right: Black chokeberry Low Scape® Mound

Below: Creeping St. John's wort

Below, right: Blue holly 'Honey Maid,' Andalusia Historic House and Garden, Andalusia, Pennsylvania

The variegated blue holly 'Honey Maid' is consistent in its variegation and is a slow grower, making it an excellent low-maintenance plant.

The golden flowers on creeping St. John's wort attract pollinators. The low stature of the plant and its thick growth make it impenetrable to weeds.

Plants for the Multi-Dimensional Hedge

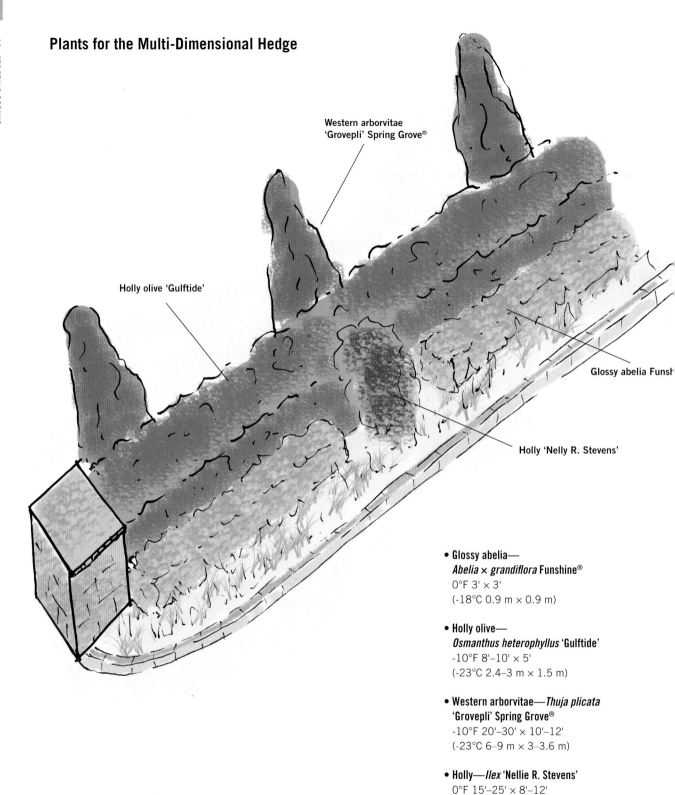

Western arborvitae
‘Grovepli’ Spring Grove®

Holly olive ‘Gulftide’

Glossy abelia Funsh

Holly ‘Nelly R. Stevens’

- Glossy abelia—
  Abelia × grandiflora Funshine®
  0°F 3' × 3'
  (-18°C 0.9 m × 0.9 m)

- Holly olive—
  Osmanthus heterophyllus ‘Gulftide’
  -10°F 8'–10' × 5'
  (-23°C 2.4–3 m × 1.5 m)

- Western arborvitae—*Thuja plicata*
  ‘Grovepli’ Spring Grove®
  -10°F 20'–30' × 10'–12'
  (-23°C 6–9 m × 3–3.6 m)

- Holly—*Ilex* ‘Nellie R. Stevens’
  0°F 15'–25' × 8'–12'
  (-18°C 4.5–7.6 m × 2.4–3.6 m)

Mixed Hedge

In Chapter 8, I discuss the history of hedges and hedgerows. It's here that we discover the importance of diversity with the early hedgerow systems. In the example on the opposite page, you will see a great depth and height of the hedging. The evergreen barrier provides a year-round wall from those passing by while also providing a strong wind block that protects the interior garden, creating a microclimate that did not exist before.

Layers of hedge plantings are more effective than solitary species of hedge. Layers provide greater depth of habitat, and the interlaced branches protect small birds from predators. Holly olive 'Gulftide' is ideal to keep the unwanted out—including deer, if you have problems with them. The leaves have spines, and it's a tough evergreen. The fall blooms release a sweet heavenly scent, making another pollinator frenzy before the winter sets in. The lower hedge is glossy abelia Funshine® that will bloom from May through frost, providing pollinators a continual food supply.

The largest of the hedges provides a bit more visual diversity. The tall hedges in the back are Western arborvitae Spring Grove®, and they add to the overall dimension of the hedge by pulling it back into the open space behind. Holly 'Nellie R. Stevens' pulls the hedge outward and becomes an exclamation point in the middle of the long hedge. Plus, it produces a great berry display for winter and becomes a prominent focal point.

Top: Glossy abelia Funshine®

Bottom: Holly olive 'Gulftide'

CHAPTER 6

PRUNING FOR STRUCTURE, SHAPE, FORM, AND PROFIT

After you've selected and planted the best shrubs for your conditions, it's time to turn your focus to pruning.

Most people treat pruning shrubs as a "one-size-fits-all" process, but nothing could be further from the truth. Not all shrubs are created equal. Their budding and bloom times vary widely and, depending on whether the plant blooms on old wood or new wood, pruning times will vary. Shrub pruning typically revolves around the plant's bloom cycle, which is interrupted when the plant is pruned at the wrong time of year. Pruning at the wrong time can also set up an unhealthy situation for the shrub by forcing new growth before frost and not giving it ample time to harden off. The new growth then becomes vulnerable to cold temperatures, and on the coldest winter days the shrub is more likely to suffer damage. You may notice the shrubs have dead branches toward their tips after a long cold winter. Or you may notice the shrub is blooming on the inside of the shrub but not on the outer branches. This is another sign that the plant was pruned at the wrong time of the plant's bloom cycle.

Pruning is an art form, not a race to the finish. Considerable thought should go into why you are pruning and how this will enhance the shrub's air flow, internal light exposure, and overall form. Each shrub has its own characteristics and charm that make it unique. When visually assessing the plant, look at its natural shape—does it have graceful, arching branches or a stiff, upright form? By studying the plant, you will learn what the plant needs to provide the best visual performance. Cutting all shrubs into "meatballs" does not allow the plants to show off their incredible natures. Pruning is not a one-size-fits-all action. Pruning is a lesson in visual observation. Which begs the question: Why do we prune shrubs in the first place?

The Three Ds of Pruning

As you'll come to learn, the reasons for pruning are many, but these primary reasons are known as the three Ds: disease, damage, and death.

• **DISEASE**—A plant with disease might show numerous symptoms, such as wilt, rot, discoloration, or deformation. Removal of the diseased portion often reduces

Shrubs growing in their natural shapes with little pruning needed. The various leaf sizes create a beautifully textured palette.

An example of rose rosette disease

the spread of the disease and prevents the complete loss of the plant. A good example of a shrub disease is rose rosette disease, which causes deformed growth of the rose's foliage. Diseased canes are misshapen and exhibit an unusual reddish coloring. If the disease is discovered early enough, the diseased cane can be pruned off at ground level. This disease is spread by a small mite, and by removing the branch, you might prevent the disease from spreading to the rest of the plant. Pruning tools need to be sharp and clean, and when pruning diseased shrubs, the tools should be thoroughly cleaned after pruning one shrub and beginning another to prevent the spread of the disease to other plants via infected tools.

- **DAMAGE**—Sometimes shrubs get damaged by a storm, heavy snowfall, or some other physical action. Removing damaged branches promptly helps prevent disease and further damage from occurring. Just like humans, when you tend to an injury quickly, there's a better chance of a speedy recovery.

- **DEATH**—Removal of dead branches after a severe winter or drought opens up the plant for more air movement and light needed to encourage new growth.

General Pruning for Performance

In addition to the three Ds, other reasons for pruning are aesthetics, the need for rejuvenation, to improve flowering or fruiting, or if a plant is sited in the wrong spot. In many cases, the latter is the number one reason pruning needs to be done—the wrong plant was planted in the wrong place and grew too large for the site. When planting shrubs, they should be planted with their maximum size in mind to keep pruning to a minimum. Plant breeders are always looking for smaller and more compact plants to reduce work for the gardener. Compact plants do not need to be pruned unless they exhibit one of the three Ds or need to be rejuvenated due to patchy growth or poor blooming (more on rejuvenating pruning in a later section). If you're interested in reducing pruning needs, look for plants that are bred for compact stature, slow growth, and consistent form.

Yellow twig dogwood (*Cornus sericea* 'Flaviramea') will have its oldest stems removed to the ground using the selective thinning technique to maintain the beautiful, vibrant yellow branches, which occur on new growth.

Selective Pruning

There are three main types of selective pruning:

- Thinning out/selective thinning
- Heading back (also called shearing)
- Rejuvenating pruning

There are also many specialty forms of pruning, such as espalier, coppicing, directional pruning, and others to be discussed in later sections. But for now, let's take a look at why and how to perform the three main types of selective pruning.

Thinning Out/Selective Thinning

The act of thinning out a shrub involves the judicious removal of some of the branches back to a main or side branch or, in some cases, all the way down to the ground. It's performed to maintain the natural shape and structure of the shrub, to limit its growth, to improve its fruiting and flowering, and to increase the amount of light that reaches its inner branches. How often you need to selectively thin a shrub depends on many factors. With selective thinning, the rule of thumb is not to remove more than one-third of the branches at a time in order to maintain good plant health and vigor.

Here is an example of
how to thin a shrub.

Heading Back (Also Called Shearing)

Shearing or heading back removes only the
terminal portion of the growing stems, encouraging them to produce side branches.
Unfortunately, this pruning method is
way overused. It has become the fallback
method for those who don't know how
to properly prune most shrubs. Instead of
selectively thinning or reducing a plant,
some people use a hedge trimmer or loppers to shear back all their shrubs, often
forming "meatball" shapes. This is not the

best pruning technique for the vast majority of shrubs because it doesn't allow for the
natural structure of the plant, and it often
causes a lot of undue stress on the plant.
Heading back is, however, the best pruning
method for hedges, which will be discussed
in greater detail in Chapter 8.

Rejuvenating Pruning

When trimming older shrubs, a more
prudent approach to pruning is necessary,
especially if the shrub has not been pruned
on a regular basis. As mentioned before,
not all shrubs are created equal, and older
shrubs can be less resilient. I have seen
many beautiful old shrubs destroyed by
aggressive pruning practices. Again, there
is no one-size-fits-all approach.

When people buy new homes, the first
thing some do to their landscape is remove
all the old plants and start with a clean
slate. Unfortunately, many people do not
see the inherent value in old plants, nor
do they know what to do with them. Some
folks are too impatient to wait to see results over time. Instant gratification does
not always lead to the best landscapes. In

This illustration shows
the before and after for
selectively thinning a
shrub with many stems.
Crossed branches
and branches growing
inward should be
removed first.

These illustrations show the before and after of rejuvenating an old shrub by removing up to one-third of the stems. Start by removing any of the crisscrossing branches and oldest stems, along with branches that are growing inward. In this process, new branches are encouraged to come up from the roots and are encouraged to grow outward. If you use this method, a two- or three-year cycle of pruning is ideal.

fact, like wine, landscapes get better with age. This doesn't mean you should never remove old plants; some may actually need to be removed because they are too far gone to be revived, or they are in the wrong location. Instead of complete removal, I recommend giving an old specimen a new life, because it may be far more valuable than you realize.

Rejuvenating pruning requires the selective removal of stems all the way down to the base of the plant, sometimes in stages (one-third at a time), and sometimes all at once. The removal of whole branches encourages the production of new growth, and while it may seem drastic, it's the best way to "freshen up" overgrown shrubs.

When to Prune

When to prune depends on many factors, including whether the plant is deciduous or evergreen and its time of bloom.

Pruning deciduous shrubs is easiest in the wintertime when you can see the individual branches. This reveals the complete structure of the plant, which helps you decide which branches to remove. However, for shrubs that bloom in the early spring, such as lilac, forsythia, pieris, viburnum, and many others, a winter pruning means you'll be cutting off all of the spring bloom. A good rule of thumb is to prune flowering shrubs as soon as they're finished blooming. That way you won't be removing the next season's blooms.

You will never feel more empowered as when you make your first pruning decisions and begin the process. The initial cuts are the most difficult, and after that you will become a pro. Remember that pruning is an art form and should not be rushed. (See the section on proper pruning cuts and the best tools for the job toward the end of this chapter.)

A Case Study in Rejuvenating an Old Shrub

The Ozark or vernal witch hazel (*Hamamelis vernalis*) in these photos was pruned between 2007 and 2013 to get the plant back into shape after a long period of time with no maintenance.

Several horticulture classes at the Ambler Arboretum participated in the pruning and learned the importance of maintaining older specimens. The process began in 2007, and by 2009 you can see the Ozark witch hazel has already had many pruning cuts that were healing from the first 2 years of class work. The first photo shows that the plant still needs additional pruning. If the branches had been pruned at an earlier age, this structural pruning would not be necessary. The targeted branches are those that are crisscrossing. In some instances, the branches have grafted themselves together or have rubbed each other so much that there are cankers (sores) that need removal.

As you can see in the upper right photo, there is a massive amount of new growth by 2011. From all the sucker growth we could select new structural branches for future training. Notice how the shrub looks like it is divided in two. We corrected the problem as we carried out the next spring's pruning.

In 2011, we removed sucker growth and some additional internal crisscrossing branches. Notice we were pruning in the fall—typically this is the wrong time to prune because the flower blooms are already developed, but structural pruning is more important in this case, and the blooms were sacrificed in order to get the plant back on a regular pruning schedule.

In 2013, we removed branches for forcing indoors (A). After the bloom was faded in early spring, we went in to thin out and do directional pruning to close the gap in the middle of the plant (B). The Ozark witch hazel was then ready to be put back on a regular pruning cycle of every other year.

Pruning cuts from the two previous years of work, 2007 to 2009

Removal of lower growth and some interior thinning out, 2011

Crisscrossing branches are targeted

By pruning, these we will force branches to fill in gaps, 2013

Before and After

The following examples show before and after of pruning a Chinese tree lilac (*Syringa reticulata* subsp. *pekinensis*), which could be a large shrub or small tree depending on how it's pruned. Students learning pruning techniques removed all crisscrossing branches, suckers, and broken limbs. They also opened the canopy with directional pruning and thinning cuts. An annual checkup will keep the shrub in check. Morris Arboretum, University of Pennsylvania, Philadelphia, Pennsylvania.

Below, left: Dog rose bejeweled in fruit

Deadheading

The removal of flowers after they bloom often encourages additional blooming from the plant if it is capable of reblooming that same season or if it is setting bloom for the next season. Deadheading is, in essence, a type of pruning. Reblooming roses are good examples of shrubs that should be deadheaded. If there is no second bloom and you deadhead anyway, you'll be preventing fruit and seed from developing. Keep in mind that you'll want to avoid deadheading if you want your shrub to produce decorative fruits or berries.

Many of the newer reblooming plants have "self-cleaning" genetics, which means the flower heads drop on their own and do not require deadheading. Most of the time these plants do not produce seed, which makes it easy for the flower to fall off at the abscission layer of the peduncle (stem of the flower) and the stem. The developing seed heads sometimes hold onto the flowers for a short time before the petals drop.

Plants that hold onto their spent blooms can look a little less than desirable. This can happen with some spiraeas, roses, and other plants. Deadheading prevents the spread of unwanted seedlings from growing in the garden. Pruning off the spent flowers right after they finish blooming is the best time to do this task.

Above: After this bud blooms on the Piedmont rhododendron (*Rhododendron minus*), pinch out the old bloom to prevent seed set. This action will force out the side buds to create flower buds to bloom instead of leafing out.

Top: Japanese spiraea
DOUBLE PLAY® CANDY
CORN® creates soft
mounds.

Below: Japanese spiraea
'Gold Mound' is one
shrub variety that needs
no pruning.

Sometimes No Pruning is Required at All

Shrub varieties that need little or no pruning have special characteristics that make them ideal for low-maintenance gardening. Perhaps they have a dwarf form or a naturally smaller stature. The only time these shrubs need pruning is if they exhibit any of the three Ds.

Contrary to what some people may believe, plants can touch each other and do not need to be pruned just to keep them from touching. This is one of the most common mistakes in the landscaping profession today. Some people use large hedge shears to scalp plants to make sure no leaves and branches

touch one another. Then they apply a heavy layer of mulch. This is not how to treat your plants. It's plant abuse. Shrub plantings look best when the plants are allowed to billow or spread, touching each other and forming mounds in the landscape. Mulch is a good thing when helping to establish plants.

Looking for a Creeper?

Sometimes creeping shrubs are needed as a groundcover to protect the soil on slopes or prevent weeds. One slow-growing creeper that has a dense habit is singleseed juniper (*Juniperus squamata* 'Blue Star'). The blue-green foliage provides a wonderful cooling effect on the hottest of days in the garden. The foliage is all awl (needle-like growth) and has a white or glaucous appearance. It's wonderful in containers with its clean appearance—no pruning necessary. In one arboretum a fifty-year-old plant was only 3 feet (0.9 m) wide.

Singleseed juniper 'Blue Star' is a slow grower.

Larger shrubs can have similar endearing traits and rarely need pruning. I can't emphasize enough that picking the right plant for the right place is key to your success in the garden, ultimately yielding a low-maintenance, relaxing haven.

A Rule of Thumb for Plant Growth

• 6" (15 cm) or less of growth per year is classified as slow

• 6" to 12" (15 to 30 cm) is considered a medium or moderate grower

• 12" (30 cm) or greater is considered a fast grower

Depending on the species, some plants will grow very slow when juvenile and faster with middle age, then will grow slow again as they get older. Other plants can be fast growers when they are young and become slow to medium growers with age, and so on. Genetics, lighting, temperature, moisture, and soil conditions all play a part in the overall rate of plant growth.

An alleé of crape myrtle at the Dallas Arboretum and Botanical Garden, Dallas, Texas, creates a cooling effect.

Specialty Pruning Techniques
Creating an Alleé

Specialty pruning can create amazing structures and visual focal points. Creating an alleé should begin with younger plants that can be pruned to force the growth upward, and later outward, eventually creating the desired tunnel effect. The lower limbs and some side limbs are selectively pruned as the plants grow upward. This is called directional pruning. Alleés are creative endeavors that are time-consuming at first but gratifying once they reach their maximum height and fulfill the desired effect. In the alleé above at the Dallas Arboretum and Botanical Garden, crape myrtle (*Lagerstroemia indica*) creates a structure that provides a cooling effect in the hot summers of Dallas. Protection from the sun and rain inspires magical moments. The stems appear sculptural with their smooth mottled bark. They feel like silk.

Starting with young plants is not always the case. In the next photo you will see how the pruning cuts were made over time to structurally develop the alleé. You can see that this was once a hedge of crape myrtle before it was turned into an alleé (or perhaps the plants had been headed back in the nursery). The thick knotting effect is often caused by heading back. There's a common saying in the industry that heading back is a form of "crape murder"!

This photo shows the cuts made over time to create the arching structure at the Dallas Arboretum and Botanical Garden in Dallas, Texas.

1. This alleé was once a hedge or had been headed back or topped. You can see the knotted growth in these areas (A).
2. They removed all the excess growth and selected the branches for top growth (B). They thinned and also did directional pruning.
3. The selected canopy branches are left to grow upward (C).
4. To make this an alleé, some large limbs at the base were removed from the inside (D), which helped to thicken the remaining ones that fashion the arching branch effect. These are classified as thinning cuts and directional cuts. Notice how the base branches are facing outward.
5. Now the only time they prune is for the three Ds. The beautiful hot-pink blooms can be seen as you approach the alleé in mid- to late summer.

Below, left and right:
The chastetree alleé
looks sculptural,
cooling, and inviting—
and the flower is
fragrant.

Japanese crape myrtle (*Lagerstroemia
fauriei*) is better suited for alleés in colder
climates. The plant yields similar results,
but an added benefit is the amazing burnt-
red-brown bark. Japanese crape myrtle has

been crossed with crape myrtle to yield
hardier cultivars, of which there are many.
The cultivars range in height from 1 foot
to 25 feet (0.3 to 7.6 m) tall like the two
species illustrated. The flowers come in a
range of colors (white, pink, rose, lavender,
and red), and there are numerous dark foliage forms in the marketplace.

The chastetree (*Vitex agnus-castus*) alleé
at the Dallas Arboretum and Botanical
Garden provides an alluring serpentine
path that has the feel of mysticism. The
twisted trunks provide a less formal feel
along the snaking pathway. Walking underneath the lower canopy allows you to
smell the blue fragrant blooms. This medicinal plant was once grown in monaster-
ies and convents in Europe in the middle
ages. It was thought that the berries and
the tea made from the leaves could ensure
chastity—hence its common name.

Persian ironwood (*Parrotia persica*), with
its mottled bark, carries a stately elegance
that makes the plant ideal for an alleé. The

Right: Persian ironwood in fall color

Below: Persian ironwood is ideal for creating an inviting alleé. Photo taken at Chanticleer Garden in Wayne, Pennsylvania.

late-winter blooms are a red-maroon hue, and the fall color is a range of yellow to orange to red.

Persian ironwood is a plant to watch in the next decade as new cultivars come out in the trade. The plant is underutilized despite its amazing attributes. It's in the witch hazel family.

Pruning for a View

If you have large shrubs that have grown thick and lush but are blocking a view, it may be time to consider pruning to open the view you want. A good way to begin the task is to check out all the positions from which you would like to see the desired view. An example might be looking out over a deck or balcony. Perhaps you want to see a water feature or a children's play area, or maybe a favorite piece of artwork or landmark. Focal points provide dimension and interest within the garden setting. Make a quick sketch of where the views should be and then look at the shrubs that need pruning. Mark the branches you think will need to be removed before actually removing anything. Study the directions of the larger internal branches— perhaps you only need to remove a partial branch. The study beforehand helps you to gain confidence in your pruning, and it provides a connection between you and the plant. You will be amazed at how well this technique works. A simple study prevents making the wrong cuts to branches. Remember, once a branch is gone, it can't be glued back on. It's better to go slow and steady to accomplish the task.

Framing a view makes focal points more apparent. It can highlight a new perspective in the garden area or make your garden

Above: This tranquil scene shows well-orchestrated planning and pruning to open the view. Photo taken at Lewis Ginter Botanical Garden, Richmond, Virginia.

Right: Japanese crape myrtle is a perfect size in relation to the house at Tyler Arboretum in Media, Pennsylvania.

Mark the branches you want to remove. Then, remove these three branches (A, B, and C) to clear the view of the peaked roof.

Remove any crisscrossing branches (D, E, F, G, H, and I)— these are best seen in winter.

feel like it goes on forever. After you have completed your initial view pruning, subsequent pruning will be easier.

By learning how to prune for a view, you will be more mindful of what and how you are planting and what views you would like to focus on.

By removing selected branches, the overall view of this home becomes more defined. The picture above shows the process.

Espaliers

Espaliers require a special form of pruning that controls a plant growing against a wall, a fence, or any other support system that keeps the plant on a two-dimensional plane. Espaliers date back to time immemorial; they're used to make fruit trees more productive and accessible when harvesting the fruits.

The example to the right is classified as a spray or splayed design—the plant is more naturalized in appearance.

The illustrations above show two of the many forms of espaliers that can be utilized when training a tree or shrub. The first is a cordon using straight lines to train the plant on a frame or trellis. The term *cordon* comes from the military usage of the word meaning a straight line. Frameworks can be constructed on walls using anchor bolts secured into the masonry. A thick-gauge wire is attached to the hooks, and the plant is then trained to grow up the structure. Planting a small shrub or tree is the easiest way to begin, because you have time to work with the plant and force the plant through a series of stem and bud cuts. When the plant is young and vigorously growing, the training may have to be carried out several times a year. As the plant gets older and the trunk and structural branches are established, less work is needed.

The second diagram is a spray or splayed design that can also be attached to a wall.

It is less formal in nature, but it yields a beautiful result, especially with shrubs like camellias (*Camellia* spp.) and roses (*Rosa* spp.).

The branches are attached to the systems using wire that is malleable, such as copper wire. As the plant grows in girth the wires are loosened so as not to girdle (or "choke") the stems. As the stems get older and woodier, the structure will retain its form and will no longer need to be wired. Raffia is another excellent material to use for tying. In the series of pictures on pages 110 and 111, you will see how a nectarine (*Prunus persica* var. *nectarina*) develops on metal fencing. Each flower or group of flowers is secured with raffia to make sure the fruit stays in place when it begins to develop and won't be pulled down by its weight as it ripens.

If you are interested in following up on espalier techniques, there are many books on the topic.

Opposite: Espaliered nectarine in bloom

Right: The nectarine is secured to the espalier frame with raffia—seen to the left in the photo.

Far right: A nectarine fruit with leaves trimmed away for better ripening. Photos taken at Longwood Gardens, Kennett Square, Pennsylvania.

Bottom: An espaliered fig located in the formal garden at George Washington's Mount Vernon, Mount Vernon, Virginia

NECTARINE
Prunus persica
var. *nucipersica*
'Early Rivers'

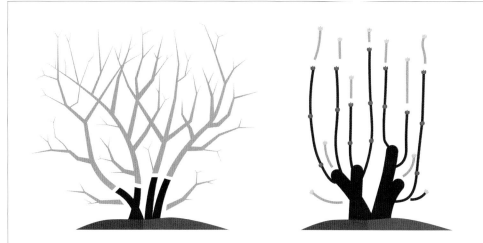

Severe Pruning Methods

In the above left illustration, a shrub has had all of its major branches removed to just above ground level. The technique encourages new growth in plants that are typically vigorous growers. It's not recommended for slow growers or older shrubs, unless done in stages. Red twig dogwood (*Cornus sericea*), bloodtwig dogwood (*Cornus sanguinea*), and swamp or silky dogwood (*Cornus amomum*) are all good examples of shrubs that are resilient enough to come back quickly after pruning using this method. For these shrubs, hard pruning like this guarantees brilliantly colored stems, which is one of the most desired traits of these types of dogwoods.

In the above right illustration, the pruning technique used is called *stooling*. It encourages new growth in an upright fashion. Stooling refers to the height of the pruning cuts, which are equivalent to the height of a footstool. Stooling is typically done each year to encourage vertical growth.

Right: Smoketree (*Cotinus coggygria* 'Velvet Cloak') has been stooled to create a wonderful backdrop for the long perennial border at Longwood Gardens, Kennett Square, Pennsylvania.

Bud and Candle Pruning for Evergreens

Bud and candle pruning are easy to do and take far less time than pruning back entire branches on evergreens. The bud and candle are two different stages of growth. The bud is the young, terminal growing point that has not yet grown. The candle is the elongated bud after it begins to grow and develop. They look just like candles on the branches of the trees.

The only difference between pruning buds and pruning candles is the age and stages at which you are pruning. These techniques are also used in bonsai, nursery production (to train whips or young tree saplings), and fruit production. Candle pruning is specific for shrubs in the pine family (Pinaceae). The candle is cut to the desired length. This forces the production of side buds to make the plant fuller for the coming year.

The term "nip it in the bud" comes from this pruning technique. Bud pruning is a good way to control growth early on. Instead of doing thinning cuts later in a plant's life, do bud thinning on a regular basis.

Once you try bud and candle pruning, you will have a new appreciation for the power of a little bud. It can change the entire future of the plant and decrease your overall workload.

This illustration shows what the tip of an evergreen branch looks like after the removal of the center bud before the bud has a chance to grow into a candle. Pinching out the center bud before it has a chance to elongate encourages new buds to form on the sides of the original bud, making the plant bushier in appearance. Pines have a strong terminal dominance that suppresses the side buds. But once the terminal bud is removed, the side buds are encouraged to grow. This task should be completed in late winter or early spring.

By cutting the candle in half, multiple buds are encouraged to develop, which will make the plant fuller in appearance and reduce the overall height of the shrub or tree.

Spruces have buds at each of the tips of the branches. When pruning spruce, remove all the tips of buds to encourage a bushier, fuller plant.

Buds have been removed from the spruce, encouraging side buds to grow.

A Case Study in Pine Pruning

Japanese black pine 'Thunderhead' (*Pinus thunbergii* 'Thunderhead') has a spreading habit that is attractive in any garden. Its beautiful crisp, clean-looking buds and candles are distinguishing features on the plant and in the landscape during the winter months (plus, they are a key ID feature). The overall growth of the plant is very compact. In order to prune the plant, perform bud removal.

Right: Removing all side buds or candles will force the central candle upward, creating a less compact growth form.

Left: Removing the central candle and two outside buds, the three buds will grow outward in a splayed pattern, reducing height.

Pruning a Spreading Conifer

When pruning horizontal, spreading plants, prune mid-way up the branch to enhance growth. New buds form behind the cut, allowing for additional growth in numerous directions. In the diagram at right, you can see that branches of the plant have been pruned halfway up the branch. When making the cuts, angle your pruner toward the end of the branch so the exposed side of the cut faces the ground and you will not see it when looking at the plant. No one will ever know that you were pruning, and your plants will look great while you wait for them to thicken up.

Russian arborvitae (*Microbiota decus-*

sata) happens to be a great groundcover. After a heavy winter, branches may die back and need some TLC. Pruning with the method just discussed will help to fill in the plant's bare spots. Note: Information on pruning hedges and topiary is found in Chapter 8.

Pruning branches halfway encourages new buds and growth.

Tools for the Task of Pruning

Before you prune, make sure you have the proper tools for the job. For shrubs and hedges, consider purchasing hand pruners, loppers, a handsaw, hedge shears, and a pole saw. Try to buy the best tools you can afford. They'll last longer as you continue to maintain your plants over the years. Not all tools are created equal. Consider how they are assembled and what type of metal they are forged from. Tools should be easy to clean and easy to sharpen. They should have replaceable blades and be comfortable to handle. Ergonomics is the most important consideration when purchasing tools. High-quality tools undergo rigorous scrutiny for ergonomics and durability before they are sold to the general public. Professional-grade tools are always an option and are found at garden centers and commercial tool sites online. When used properly, your tools should be comfortable to use. Comfort is essential to prevent carpal tunnel syndrome, neck and back aches, and so forth.

Here are some essential tools for your tool collection.

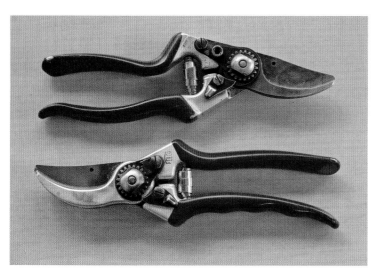

▲ Bypass pruners are a must for the gardener. If you purchase a cover (sheath) for the pruners, you will be able to conveniently attach them to your pants or to a tool belt. Bypass pruners make a nice clean cut. Make sure that your tools are sharpened regularly.

▶ Learning how to sharpen your tools with files and stones like these is as easy as looking online at YouTube instruction videos. Sharpening your own tools will save you a good deal of time and money. Whether it's your pruners or your lawn mower blades, sharp tools prevent ripping and tearing of the plant tissue. Unsharpened tools lead to a greater chance of injury to the plant or to yourself.

▶ Loppers are a step up from pruners. They are capable of pruning larger-diameter stems. Loppers allow you to reach farther into the plant. Telescoping loppers have extendable handles for extra reach. Loppers also come with ratchet action, which applies less pressure on your elbows and arms. These are invaluable for pruning larger limbs on shrubs. Very little pressure needs to be applied to make the desired cut.

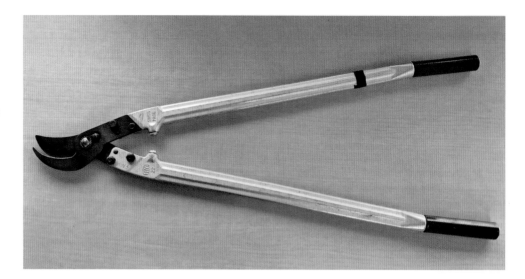

▶ Handsaws come in various types, including collapsible or with stationary blades. Collapsible saws are great for branches that your pruners and loppers can't cut. A good sharp saw is a must for large branch removal. Keep in mind that you will always be using the three-point pruning method described in the next section.

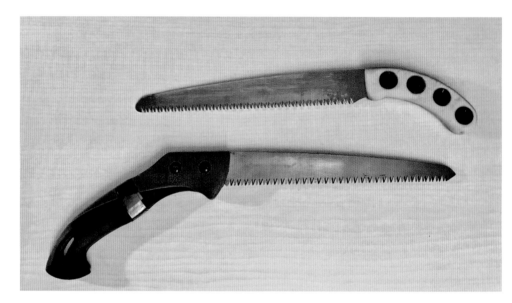

▶ Pole saws are used in the same manner as handsaws, but you will be reaching above your head to remove the branches. Be sure to wear a helmet when working with overhead pruning equipment in case a branch drops accidentally. Eye protection and gloves should always be worn too!

▶ When pruning small shrubs, hedge shears work well. They allow you to get into tight places and low to the ground. If you are doing a large hedge, electric hedge shears are ideal. Many professionals prefer the battery-operated ones because they are lighter and quieter, and there are no fumes to breathe in. When working with any power tools, gloves, eye protection, and ear protection are a must.

▲ What needs to be said about chain saws: Injuries are rampant! Protective gear is essential, including Kevlar pants, eye protection, head protection, gloves, ear protection, and sturdy shoes. Be aware of the saw's kickback zone, which is located at the top tip of the saw blade. Injuries can be prevented if safety is foremost in mind. If you are not certain how to use a chain saw, you can take classes on using power equipment. Or when purchasing you can ask for a demo in safe practices. Chain saws are typically used when a handsaw is too small for the job. Battery-pack chain saws are a great way to reduce noise and lighten the load, especially when holding the equipment for long periods of time. Chain saws should be sharpened regularly (professional sharpeners are best). Do not use power tools without having someone else at home, just in case the unthinkable happens.

When it comes to pruning, always make sure you have the right tool for the task. Have a work plan before you begin. Wear sturdy shoes, comfortable gloves, and pants. Wear eye protection so no debris gets in your eyes. And be sure to protect your ears from loud noise.

Making Proper Pruning Cuts

This diagram shows how, and how not, to prune shrubs.

This example is the proper way to prune by cutting on a slight angle and leaving a bit of space above the bud.

This cut exposes too much of the interior of the plant to the atmosphere, where it becomes more vulnerable to disease and desiccation. It's also harder for the plant to heal.

The lowest point on the cut in this example sits below the bud on the opposite side. This makes the bud vulnerable to desiccation and freezing, especially when pruned later in the season.

This cut is too far from the bud. The node (where the bud is located) is rich in meristematic cell growth and allows for quick healing to occur. The farther away the cut is made from the node, the more difficult it is for the plant to move hormones to that area for healing. Typically, this form of cut dies back above the bud and makes the plant unsightly, while also making the plant more vulnerable to disease.

Tool Care

Cleaning your tools prolongs the life of your tool investment. Use disinfectant wipes or a disinfectant spray for cleaning your tools. Wipes are especially nice to use while out in the field and they are reusable. Clean tools thoroughly after your work sessions. If you are pruning any diseased areas on your plants, clean your tools in between each plant so as not to carry any unwanted disease to the next plant. A small spray can of olive oil is good to keep on hand to oil any tool parts that need lubrication. Now you are good to go.

Three-Point Cut

The three-point cut is used when removing limbs that are large but can still be cut with a handsaw. To reduce the excess weight on the branch base before the final cut is taken, the largest part of the branch is removed, first with an under cut and then with an over cut. The final cut is made just outside the branch collar.

Second cut—over cut all the way through to reduce the weight from the branch

First cut—under cut part way through the branch

Third cut—final cut just outside the branch collar

Pruning for Profit

After having a flower shop for over twelve years, one gets to know the value in having cut flowering branches that are harvested locally. If you love to prune and you're great at it, you might want to consider pruning for profit. All too often valuable cut stems are put right into the chipper; this is especially true around Christmas when limbs are being pruned off conifers. These are chipped while florists are paying a premium to have greens trucked across the country from suppliers. Branches cut locally can go right into the trade if they are bundled by weight or metric stem counts. If advance notice is given to a wholesaler or retailer about a select conifer, it could even be sold before the plant is pruned. Getting more creative, what about selling to business districts that decorate their storefronts for winter? Or why not prune hedgerows in late winter for forced flowering branches such as forsythia or quince?

What about starting your own flower farm to cultivate amazing plants for clients in the cut flower market? Anticipating client needs—including their future potential and their desire for the unusual—can continually increase the scope of your business. Study trends, investigate flower shops, visit locations in the off season, and

Border forsythia 'Beatrix Farrand' is a floral favorite for spring arrangements.

A young showy panicle hydrangea 'Limelight'

There are many exceptional stems for cutting. I already alluded to holiday greens and spring bloomers, but there are other blooming woody shrubs that are fabulous for party and wedding work. These include the panicle hydrangea 'Limelight' (*Hydrangea paniculata* 'Limelight'), which has large robust flowers that hold up beautifully once they firm up on the plant. In general, all panicle hydrangeas have great potential for the market, and there are so many different cultivars with different forms and color variations—from white to cream, and green to pink tones. Harvest the long-stemmed, fresh flower heads for arrangements and party work, while using shorter-stemmed varieties for bouquets, dried arranging, and wreath making. Panicle hydrangeas flower on new wood, which will provide large numbers of consistent stems for cutting.

There are many other hydrangeas that can be used as cut stems, including bigleaf hydrangea (*Hydrangea macrophylla*) and smooth hydrangea (*Hydrangea arborescens*) (see pages 66 to 71). The color ranges of both species provide a wonderful diversity for the floral designer. Keep in mind that bigleaf hydrangeas are best purchased as rebloomers—such as those in the END-LESS SUMMER® line. That's right—not all bigleaf hydrangeas are rebloomers. In case the winter weather affects the previous season's buds, you will still have a crop on the new wood varieties. Flowers from all three hydrangeas can be dried and sold.

be observant. Start a consortium of growers and work together to grow cut flowers and greens for the trade. Having numerous outlets for your cut stems is key. Consider selling to specialty supermarkets, wholesalers, interior plantscapers, party planners, restaurants, caterers, and flower shops. You may even look to people who make baskets and furniture because they love to work with more unusual stems. The options are endless with great imagination and vision.

Pruning for Profit Guide

Common Name of Plant	Latin Name of Plant	Blooms on	Cutting Time Spring
Beach plum	*Prunus maritima*	Blooms on old wood	Cut in early spring before buds break and sell for forcing
Beautyberry	*Callicarpa dichotoma*	Blooms on new wood	
Bigleaf hydrangea	*Hydrangea macrophylla*	Blooms on old wood; there are reblooming lines with blooms on old and new wood	
Blue holly or Meserve holly	*Ilex* x *meserveae* 'Blue Prince'	Blooms on old wood	
Blue holly or Meserve	*Ilex* x *meserveae* 'Blue Princess'	Blooms on old wood	
Drooping laurel	*Leucothoe fontanesiana*	Blooms on old wood	Blooming stems can be cut
English holly	*Ilex aquifolium*	Blooms on old wood	
Forsythia	*Forythia* spp.	Blooms on old wood	Cut before the buds open; can cut while in tight bud; cut each stem at ground level
Panicle hydrangea	*Hydrangea paniculata*	Blooms on new wood	
Purple willow	*Salix purpurea* 'Nana'	Blooms on old wood	Cut for catkins; good for weaving waddles, baskets
Pussy willow	*Salix* spp.	Blooms on old wood	Cut stems before bud break to use in streambank plantings or for propagation; cut long stems to stool height just after the silvery buds push out and the bud scale is still intact for the cut market; cut stems for constructing structures before bud break
Red twig dogwood	*Cornus sericea*	Blooms on old wood	
Smooth hydrangea	*Hydrangea arborescens*	Blooms on new wood	
White forsythia	*Abeliophyllum distichum*	Blooms on old wood	Cut before the buds open; can cut while in tight bud; cut each stem at ground level

Cutting Time Summer	Cutting Time Fall	Cutting Time Winter	Market
Fruit harvested for jams and jellies			Flower Market, Food Market
Harvest stems in late summer when the fruits are ripe			Flower Market
Cut flower heads when they are firm to the touch if you plan on drying them; if you are using for cut flowers, cut after the flowers have fully shown color; you can cut these at ground level or 12" (30 cm) or longer	Quality declines when harvesting in the fall for drying		Flower Market
		Cut stems and sell as boxed loose product or sell by the bag by the pound; can make wreaths as soon as the holly is cut; no berries, but the foliage is beautiful	Flower Market
		Cut stems and sell as boxed loose product or sell by the bag by the pound; can make wreaths as soon as the holly is cut; berries hold up well	Flower Market
Foliage stems can be cut after they harden off	Foliage stems can be cut	Foliage stems can be cut	Flower Market
		Cut stems and sell as boxed loose product or sell by the bag by the pound; can make wreaths as soon as the holly is cut; berries hold up well	Flower Market
			Flower Market
Cut flower heads when they are firm to the touch for fresh cuts; cut for drying as they begin to turn color	Quality declines when harvesting in the fall for drying		Flower Market
			Flower Market, Craft Market
			Flower Market, Craft Market, Restoration, Other
		Cut any time after the leaves have fallen for arranging the twigs; cut in late winter for using in stream banks and for propagation	Flower Market, Craft Market, Restoration, Other
Cut flower heads when they are firm to the touch for fresh cuts; these are not always the best for drying (depends on cultivar); you can cut these at ground level or 12" (30 cm) or longer	Quality declines when harvesting in the fall for drying		Flower Market
			Flower Market

A general rule of thumb for pruning is to prune directly after flowering. This is especially true of spring bloomers. There is a 2 to 3-week-long window after spring bloom before the buds begin to develop for the following year. As mentioned earlier in this chapter, one of the biggest mistakes in pruning is to prune at the wrong time of year. If you plan to prune for profit, make sure that pruning is done at the correct time of year to maximize your yield. When selling forced flower stems for market, you will cut the stems just before the buds break, but they should be showing good color in the buds just before they burst. Some plants need at least one bud open on the stem before the others will open after cutting. Experimenting with one or two stems will help you determine the best method.

Coppicing for Cut Branches

Coppicing is a pruning technique that works with specific plants to force new straight shoot growth from the trunk when cut just above ground level. The shoots can be grown for propagation stems or for use in the cut flower market. Willows and multi-stemmed dogwoods are good examples of shrubs that do well when coppiced. Extra-long cuttings from coppices can be used for making baskets and structures. Dormant stems can be cut for riparian restoration: The stems are poked directly into streambanks to root for stabilization. For this purpose, willow or red twig dogwood are prime candidates. You can also make fascines (stems made into bundled logs) from extra-long willow stems for streambank restoration. There is a huge market for fascines in flood-prone

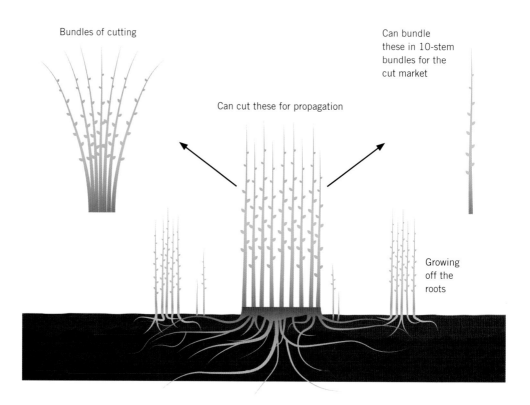

Bundles of cutting

Can bundle these in 10-stem bundles for the cut market

Can cut these for propagation

Growing off the roots

Coppiced tree or shrub can create hundreds of cuttings for propagation or for the cut flower market. It can also be used for restoration. *Salix* spp., *Cornus sericea, Cornus amomum, Cornus alba*

Above: Pussy willow (*Salix discolor*) with their catkins in bloom is a herald of spring. Before bloom, they are ideal for the flower market.

Right: Purple willow (*Salix purpurea* 'Nana') is low growing, and stems can be sold for making baskets. Longwood Gardens, Kennet Square, Pennsylvania.

areas and in areas where heavy livestock grazing is discouraged along streambanks. These "living logs" will root in place once fastened to the streambank. Cultivating shrubs for riparian restoration can be very rewarding, especially if you work with clients to customize what they need for their specific sites. If you are selling cut stems for propagation, cuttings from a coppiced stump will give you good vigorous stems for clients to root.

Purple willow (*Salix purpurea* 'Nana'), with its beautiful purple catkins, has a multitude of uses. It can be bundled for the flower market or used for making wattle fences or baskets.

Flowering quince (*Chaenomeles speciosa* 'Alba') comes in a range of colors and sizes. Forced branches of white flowering quince have wedding written all over their blooms. Flower shops and party planners will love using them from your farm. Flowering quince makes an excellent hedge too—see Chapter 8.

Fragrant, delicate, and ideal for the early border garden, white forsythia (*Abeliophyllum distichum*) is an excellent choice for the flower market—cut it in early spring just before it bursts into bloom

Left and below:
Flowering quince
(*Chaenomeles speciosa*)

Opposite: White
forsythia (*Abeliophyllum
distichum*)

CHAPTER 7

PROPAGATING SHRUBS

Propagation is a fascinating topic. It is the art and science that allows for reproductive creativity. Generating new plants for the garden can be a gratifying experience for the professional horticulturist, seasoned gardener, and amateur plant lover. If you are a professional horticulturist, propagating plants can be a desirable and lucrative activity. For the homeowner, it's about experiencing the joy of making more shrubs—for free! In the end, nurturing and increasing plant communities offers a lifetime of fulfillment.

There are two forms of propagation—asexual and sexual. Sexual propagation is the production of new plants from seed, while asexual propagation uses part of the plant—such as the stem, leaf, or a piece of the root—to create an entirely new plant. This is possible because, unlike humans, every cell in a plant contains all the genetic material necessary to create a whole new plant (a trait called totipotency) that's an exact genetic clone of the parent plant. Not all plants lend themselves well to both forms of reproduction. There are plants that reproduce asexually and scantly germinate from seed because of low fertility rates, complex dormancies that can take several years to break, or a short season that limits the success rate of newly emerging seedlings. Then there are plants that grow easily from seed but challenge gardeners when cuttings are attempted.

Asexual Reproduction

Asexual reproduction is the replication of a plant without the use of sexual parts—no flowers are involved, and no seed created. There are various means of asexual reproduction, starting with taking a simple stem cutting from a plant. By taking a cut portion of a stem and pushing into the ground, potting it up, or putting it in water, roots may develop from the stem's cells under the cutting's surface. The DNA of this plant is an exact replica of the parent.

A shrub expends less energy through asexual reproduction than it does by reproducing through flower and seed. And there is no intermingling of genetic material, so 100 percent of the parent's traits are passed on to the next generation. There are pros and cons of asexually replicating a plant repeatedly.

Virginia rose (*Rosa virginiana*) hips can be cut open and the seeds removed for planting.

THE PROS:

- Reproduction can happen rapidly, often in one growing season.
- In the case of mass marketing, the plant can be distributed nationally within several growing seasons due to the increase in the rate of production of new plants.
- Each generation is consistent with the one before. You know exactly what you're going to get.

THE CONS:

- There's no genetic diversity, which creates large monocultures of plants.
- Genetic weakness is possible. If a disease or pest happens to attack, all plants would have the same level of susceptibility.

Methods of Asexual Propagation for Shrubs
STEM CUTTINGS

Taking stem cuttings is one of the easiest ways to asexually propagate shrubs. It's important to know whether each shrub prefers to be propagated from cuttings taken from last year's woody growth or the current season's new green growth. Woody cuttings are often taken in late winter or early spring, while new-wood cuttings are best taken in late spring through fall. A good propagation handbook or website will guide you to which type of cutting is best for which species of shrub, or you can experiment and do some of both to see which is more successful.

While stem cuttings of some shrubs root easily in water (willow for example), most need to be grown in potting soil, vermiculite, or some other type of growing medium. Here's the step-by-step for growing new shrubs via stem cuttings.

MATERIALS NEEDED:

- New 3- to 4-inch (7.5 to 10 cm) plastic pots; alternatively, you can use plastic nursery trays specifically made for cutting propagation
- Sterile potting soil or vermiculite
- Sharp, disinfected pruners
- Rooting hormone (available at nurseries or from online stores)
- Clear plastic bags or domes to cover the pots or nursery tray

STEP 1: Fill the pots with potting soil or vermiculite to within ½ inch (1 cm) of their upper rim.

STEP 2: Select a shrub with robust growth. Cut portions of the stem from the branches. Each stem cutting should be 3 to 4 inches (7.5 to 10 cm) in length and should contain at least two sets of nodes (buds where the leaves emerge from the stem). The cuttings do not have to be from the terminal portion of the stem.

STEP 3: Remove all but the top-most set of leaves from each cutting.

STEP 4: Dip the bottom inch of the stem into the rooting hormone and tap off any excess. Stick the hormone-covered stem into a soil-filled pot, being careful to have good soil-to-stem contact. The uppermost set of nodes should be just above the soil surface.

STEP 5: Once all the cuttings have been inserted into a pot, water them in well and cover the pot with a clear plastic bag or dome to maintain high humidity around the cutting.

Willow cuttings after being in water for 2 weeks.

STEP 6: Place the potted cuttings in bright light. In a sunny windowsill or under grow lights is ideal. For large numbers of cuttings, a greenhouse or high tunnel is best.

STEP 7: Remove the plastic covering and water the soil when necessary. Do not allow it to dry out; doing so could damage newly emerging roots.

STEP 8: In 4 to 6 weeks, remove the plastic covering and continue to water when necessary. Most shrub cuttings form roots within 6 weeks, but some, especially hardwood cuttings, may take a good while longer.

STEP 9: Once roots have formed, remove the new plant from its pot and plant it in its new home or a larger container.

While stem cuttings are an easy way to propagate many shrubs, it can be a real challenge for certain species. Again, a good propagation handbook will have more advice on dealing with challenging species.

AIR LAYERING

Layering naturally occurs when the branches of a shrub touch the ground. The moist soil beneath the shrub helps to create the perfect environment for roots to begin to grow at the point where the soil and the stem meet. Layering is a way for the plant to propagate itself asexually, repeatedly creating identical offspring. Shrubs that are known to layer on their own are those with low, sweeping branches, including forsythia, fig, bramble, weigela, winterberry, and spiraea, to name just a few. Some species will naturally root more easily than others.

You can speed up or artificially recreate this natural process by layering the plant yourself. A broad number of shrubs can be propagated using this technique, including azaleas, rhododendrons, boxwoods, hydrangeas, shrub roses, cotoneasters, viburnums, and many more.

MATERIALS NEEDED:

- 16-gauge copper wire or equivalent, cut in 6-inch (15 cm) lengths (copper wire is used because it's flexible and won't injure the plant)
- Clean pruners
- Trowel

This common fig (*Ficus carica* 'Magnolia') has naturally generated a new plant where a branch meets the soil via a process called layering. Once roots are formed, the new fig plant can be severed from the mother plant, dug up, and moved to a new location.

1

2

3

STEP 1: Select a shrub that is robust, with lots of low-hanging branches. It's best to attempt shrub layering on a day after a rainstorm when the ground is moist in mid- to late spring.

STEP 2: Select branches that are flexible and long enough to come in contact with the soil. Each selected branch should have some old and new growth present. Since not every point of contact will develop roots, it's best to attempt this technique on multiple branches at the same time to ensure your chances of success.

STEP 3: Follow the stem back from the tip of the branch to where the older wood is found. Older wood is olivine in color and has raised lenticels or bumps on the stem; newer wood will be closer to the ends of the branches and will be green and very pliable. Remove the first set of leaves or small branchlets from the older wood by pinching or pruning them off close to the node (bud). Cutting at the node triggers the plant to start forming callus tissue.

Border forsythia 'Beatrix Farrand' (*Forsythia* × *intermedia* 'Beatrix Farrand') is an excellent candidate for propagation via layering. The low, arching branches make the job easier.

STEP 4: Loosen the soil with a trowel where the branch will make contact. Take the wire and bend it in half, like a hairpin. Place the branch against the loosened soil and push the wire into the ground, hooking it over the stem and holding it in place against the soil. Put the wire close to the node but not on top of it.

STEP 5: Cover the pinned stem with a small mound of soil. The darkness causes the callus tissue to differentiate into roots, rather than leaves.

4

5

Some sources suggest applying rooting hormone to the stem where it contacts the soil, but I find rooting hormone is not necessary, because most shrubs layer easily without it. It may, however, be necessary for plants that are more difficult to propagate using this technique.

STEP 6: In the fall, sever the new plant from the mother shrub. If layering is performed in the spring, the new plant will be fully rooted by fall. Check your pinned branches periodically throughout the summer to make sure they have enough water. If the ground is dry, water the area thoroughly. A thin layer of mulch over the soil also helps retain soil moisture. One easy way to tell when the plant is rooted is by the position of the branch tip; it will usually point upward when fully rooted. Use a sharp pair of pruners to cut the new plant away from the parent plant, dig it up, and transplant it to a permanent home.

Propagation Tip

Consider keeping a log of what you've propagated, so you'll remember where the plant came from and when you performed the process. You may also want to note where you plan to move your new shrubs once they've taken root.

1

Make three plants from one by using a spade to divide the plant at these two points.

PLANT DIVISION

Another form of asexual reproduction is plant division. Shrubs that have multiple stems coming out from the ground can usually be divided. Check the plant carefully to make sure that it does not emerge from just one point. Smooth hydrangea (*Hydrangea arborescens*) is a good shrub to divide.

In the example above, smooth hydrangea is being divided in late spring when the leaves have already emerged. Typically, divisions are done earlier in the year, but because smooth hydrangea is going to be replanted directly in the garden, it will still work, as long as it's kept well-watered.

MATERIALS NEEDED:

- Shrub in need of division
- Sharp, clean shovel
- Work gloves

STEP 1: Examine the plant and loosen the roots a bit. Study the root system and crown of the plant to determine where the divisions will take place. There are at least two places where it can be divided.

2

3

STEP 2: With a sharp spade, cut through the first section of the plant.

STEP 3: Whatever roots you can't cut with the spade, use a pair of sharp, clean hand pruners to complete the job.

STEP 4: Repeat Steps 2 and 3 to get your second new plant divided from the central portion of the plant. Now you have two new plants cut away from the parent plant.

STEP 5: Replant them right away because they are actively growing. Water the new plants well and continue to water them throughout the season until they are well established. A thin layer of mulch will help to keep the soil evenly moist.

ROOT CUTTINGS

There are many shrubs that can be asexually reproduced by taking root cuttings. This method is particularly effective for shrubs that naturally spread themselves through their root systems and pop up in various locations away from the original plant. Sumac (*Rhus* sp.), yellowroot (*Xanthorhiza simplicissima*), lowbush blueberry (*Vaccinium angustifolium*), and black chokeberry (*Aronia melanocarpa*) are all good examples. Plants that reproduce from the roots are wonderful for covering a large area and are excellent at keeping areas weed free, thereby reducing overall maintenance.

There are several ways to begin the process. You can take cuttings from plants already established in the ground or take cuttings from a container-grown plant. Following is the latter method using *Aronia melanocarpa.*

MATERIALS NEEDED:
- Parent plant
- Clean, sharp pruning shears
- Small pots filled with sterile potting soil or vermiculite

1

2

STEP 1: Remove the plant from the container and loosen the soil around the root system.

STEP 2: Cut off pieces of thicker root with a clean, sharp pair of pruners. Lay all the cuttings in the same direction to distinguish the top end from the bottom. In this case it will be easy to tell the difference because most of the roots have green top growth. However, in many cases the root pieces will not have shoots attached to them, so maintaining their polarity is important. If root cuttings are planted upside down, they will not grow.

STEP 3: Prepare the cuttings by removing any side roots. These cuttings will be potted up, but if you choose, you can replant them directly back into the garden. Mark off the area so you know where they are.

3

4

STEP 4: Fill a pot ¾ of the way up with potting soil. Place the cuttings in the container with the top of the cuttings standing in the upright position. Then cover with soil.

STEP 5: Prepare a label that includes the date, plant name, and any other information you would like to include, then write it in your Propagation Log. Now your new root cuttings are complete.

STEP 6: Once your cuttings are planted, sink the pot partway into the ground and water them in well. Keep them well watered until they are well established. Once that occurs, you can plant the new plants into the garden.

Rooted cuttings on large plants are usually done when the plant is dormant in late winter or in fall. Again, the timing will be determined by the plant.

5

1

Sexual Propagation

Seed is the result of flower fertilization. The male pollen lands on or is carried to the female stigma and begins the journey down the style of the plant until the pollen reaches the ovule in the ovary. Once the union between pollen and ovule is formed, a seed begins to grow.

Depending on the plant and the conditions, germination can be quick, without any dormancies. But some seeds may have one, two, or even three dormancies before they will germinate. Dormancy is a fail-safe mechanism for the plant, so that it doesn't germinate in cold weather, drought, or other less-than-ideal conditions. The time and dormancy for germination not only revolve around the plant's cycles, they revolve around environmental conditions, animal movement, and soil conditions as well.

Starting Shrubs from Seed

Some plants, like the hop tree (*Ptelea trifoliata*), do not have a dormancy, and seeds can be picked off the plant in early fall and planted in the greenhouse. Germination takes place over the winter, and by spring you will have sizeable plants for establishing in the garden. Other plants require a period of cold weather, or even exposure to wildfire or passage through an animal's gut, in order to break dormancy. Plant propagation handbooks and websites can offer a wealth of information about whether or not a particular shrub's seed needs to be subjected to certain conditions before it germinates. In this example, I'm using the above-mentioned shrub, since it is particularly easy to grow from seed.

2

MATERIALS NEEDED:

- Seeds
- Sterile potting soil
- 3- to 4-inch (7.5 to 10 cm) pots, new or sterilized
- Plant labels and a #2 pencil

STEP 1: Gather the seed that you want to germinate.

STEP 2: Fill a clean pot with soil almost to the top. Place the seeds in by distributing

The 1-year-old seedling the following fall

3 & 4

them evenly across the surface. In this case, the seed can be cleaned by removing the winged portion.

STEP 3: Cover the seed with soil, filling the pot nearly to the top. Do not push the soil down. When watering the seeds in, the soil will naturally settle.

STEP 4: Label the pot. Pencil does not wash or fade away over time like markers or other writing implements.

STEP 5. Insert the label into the soil with the date on the uppermost portion of the tag so you can note how long it takes to germinate. Shrub seeds can be germinated indoors over the winter if you have grow lights. By spring you will have a sizable plant to put in the garden.

If you would like to know more about seed germination, seed dormancy, etc., check out the sources on page 212.

Legalities of Propagation

Finally, if you happen to buy a patented plant (as discussed in Chapter 3), there are legalities regarding their propagation. If your plant has been patented, it will have a patent number on the plant tag. If the tag is missing or you are not sure of the plant's status, you can Google the name of the plant you purchased and see if it has a plant patent number.

If you are a homeowner interested in increasing the number of plants in your garden, you can propagate the patented plant as long as you are not growing it for resale.

How Do You Know if a Plant Is Patented?

Let's look at the pot tag for smooth hydrangea Invincibelle Mini Mauvette®. The first hint that the plant is patented is the registration symbol after the name. The botanical name comes next. After the botanical name comes the patents for this plant. In this case there are two numbers—one from the United States and the other from Canada. **Invincibelle Mini Mauvette®** *Hydrangea arborescens* **'NCHA7' USPP 30,358, Can PBRAF.**

Propagating this plant for commercial purposes is illegal. There are a set number of plants that are licensed to be propagated. If there happen to be more plants on the market than licenses, the propagator who is caught will be fined. There are "patent police," so be mindful of this illegal activity. If you want to be a licensed grower, you are obligated to contact the company of the plant's origin. Only approved qualified growers can produce or grow the patented plant. And each grower pays a fee to propagate each of the plants. This is a royalty that goes back to the developer.

Opposite: Buttonbush (*Cephanlanthus occidentalis*) seed can be collected in fall for planting.

CHAPTER 8

HEDGES AND HEDGEROWS

H edges and hedgerows each have an interesting history unto themselves. Some hedgerows are ancient structures, remnants of old-growth forest that date back millennia, when humankind's hunter-gatherer status changed to farmer. As the earliest farmers cleared the land, they left remnants of the ancient woodland to demarcate the edges of their new fields.

Farm crops produced most efficiently when planted in straight rows; the woodland edges followed these same patterns and created giant blocks surrounded by hedgerows. Small lanes were cleared between hedgerows, wide enough for a wagon to pull the crops from the field to the hamlets. Roadside hedgerows protected farmers and their newly picked crops as they traveled, keeping the valuable food store out of the sun and wind.

Farmers learned through their trials and tribulations that hedgerows prevented erosion in the fields. The green corridors provided shelter to the farmer from storms and from the sun's sweltering heat. Some bird populations remained in what was left of the ancient woods, while other species moved in to make the hedgerows home. Light from the open fields lit up the interior of the strips of woodland and provided additional opportunities for plants to grow that were unable to grow in the dark woods. The fields created a different interaction between animals and people. Along the edges of the fields, solitary bees, beetles, wasps, and flies flourished, inhabiting stems of broken plants, downed logs, and hollows in trees. Pollinators established themselves close to the blooming crops and helped pollinate the flowers, which ensured a stable food supply. Ancient humans learned to tend bees and relish the ambrosia of honey when the hives' stores were full. Over time, people began to realize that insects were invaluable to their farming.

Opposite: Bay laurel (*Laurus nobilis*) in Italy

Right: In this photo, you see the classic lane between hedgerows at RHS Garden Hyde Hall in England. The shrubs and trees are sparse from loss through the ages. In many parts of the world, hedgerows are now being replanted to restore what was lost.

Ancient peoples once observed nature like we follow our cell phones today. They watched the movement of animals, paid attention to the weather, and noted how the shade moved across the fields. They learned how to plant crops to take full advantage of the sun's warmth in the fields during the growing season. They discerned the wind patterns and noticed the protection that hedgerows provided on the windiest of days.

As farm communities grew and larger tracts of woodland disappeared from the landscape, the hedgerows became more vital for habitat and for species survival. What remained was a vast network of hedgerows and pathways. As the human population continued to grow, it became apparent that the hedgerows needed further tending. While observing animal enclosures, farmers realized that their animals needed greater protection from predators. The farm animals also needed to be discouraged from making their way through the hedgerows while they foraged on the delectable shrubs. Felled logs were added to the field side of the hedgerows. Farmers noticed that some of the stumps from the felled trees produced a new growth that was straight and shrublike. By observing this new growth, farmers learned to coppice trees to increase habitat and provide kindling for fires.

Farmers learned that a partially chopped tree could also produce flushes of new growth. The tree was chopped partway through and then pushed on an angle from its original vertical state. In so doing, the partially felled tree began to produce new growth along the trunk. This technique of partially felling trees using bill hooks for cutting and weaving the branches became

A grouping of coppiced shrubs and trees encourages new dense growth to form while also providing additional light to the floor below. Highbush blueberry (*Vaccinium corymbosum*), red maple (*Acer rubrum*), and peachleaf willow (*Salix amygdaloides*) are plants that respond well to coppicing for hedgerows.

Top: A natural type of pleached tree. Nature provides natural pleaching, like growth from this partially upended tree. The 45-degree angle encourages additional growth from the base of the tree and along its trunk, as well as from its roots to balance out the tree's pitch.

Bottom: The remains of ancient hedgerows are visible in the distance—photo taken at Hidcote Manor Garden, England.

known as *pleaching*. Between coppicing and pleaching, people learned two valuable techniques for forcing new growth. The growth created thicker and more lush hedgerows.

In the gaps of the hedgerow from the felled trees, additional light provided new opportunities for different species to grow. Brambles and other berried shrubs grew in the sunny gaps, providing additional wild food sources for animals and the early farming communities.

The ancient art of pleaching is still done today in England. Maintaining heritage hedgerows is a priority—they strongly define the English countryside and other parts of Europe.

The historic hedgerows are apparent everywhere across the countryside. Even from an airplane the signature patchwork quilt of hedgerows and fields makes the English and European landscapes identifiable. Walking the country lanes and viewing the hedgerows up close, you can see the layers of intricacy that can develop through the ages. The lanes that were nestled between the hedgerows are still an important network for travel today.

Hedgerows have influenced a bevy of writers romanticizing, villainizing, and fondly remembering their importance during World War II. Hedgerows were places where underground bunkers were built to protect the locals during the hundreds of air raids.

Hugh Barker's amazing book *Hedge Britannia* is an impassioned tribute to hedges and hedgerows. His stories pay

homage to the ancient past while valuing today's hedgerow craftsmen who continue to carry out the ancient art of pleaching using modern equipment—keeping injury to a minimum—as they reinforce and lengthen the miles of hedges that snake through the English countryside. Over time, hedgerows became more than boundaries for fields—they became boundaries for feudal states as well.

or two species, rather than having a great diversity like the old hedgerows.

Hedges and Ownership

When the feudal system collapsed and the upper gentry began parceling land to the wealthy, hedgerows took on yet another function: to delineate new private property lines. Existing hedgerows and newly planted hedges divided up open areas of the countryside and separated the gentry from the poorer folk. The new hedges that were planted by the wealthy were mostly of one

Paralleling Europe in the Colonies

Similar hedgerow techniques were brought to the early colonies by English, Dutch, Swedish, and French settlers. As America was developing, we too became a country of hedgerows. These can still be found down the small lanes of the Mid-Atlantic Region, New England, and the South. Our hedgerows were comprised

Top: This is an example of how hedges are planted now in England. Hawthorn (*Crataegus monogyna*) is the plant of choice. The flowers are white in spring, followed by small apple-like fruits that are ideal for attracting wildlife. RHS Garden Hyde Hall.

Bottom: Here you can see how one might plant a new hedge using the old techniques (minus the black wrap) to make a property boundary. This is newly planted hedging that will later be pleached at RHS Garden Hyde Hall.

Left: Female digger
wasp paralyzes prey

Right: Osage orange
with spines for hedging

of mixed hardwoods, conifers, broadleaved evergreens, brambles, blooming shrubs, perennials, and annuals.

Hedges and hedgerows were wonderful windbreaks—they helped to keep snow on the fields and off the lanes in the colonies. They were sinks of diversity and important animal corridors. They also provided sources of food and medicinals. Insect pollinators lived in the hedgerows and ensured crops were pollinated. Some insects, like the great golden digger wasp (*Sphex ichneumoneus*), helped to pollinate and killed harmful insects that plagued the farmers' crops.

An important technique learned from the Osage Indians helped French settlers build hedgerow enclosures of osage orange (*Maclura pomifera*) to contain and protect their animals. Remains of these osage orange hedges can still be found along small country roads on the East Coast and in the Midwest. Osage can asexually reproduce from its roots, which is why it made a great hedging plant. When coppiced or stooled, it forced more sucker growth from the trunk and roots to provide a thick impenetrable hedge, spines and all. These new hedge borders had to be trimmed in order to be kept in check. As fencing was created later on in history, trimming was no longer necessary. Today, tall unpruned osage orange trees can be found growing down narrow roads, dropping their large bright-green fruit in the fall—remnants of a bygone era.

Hedgerows vs. Hedges

The distinction between hedgerows and hedges is important: Hedgerows are wild, natural borders, whereas hedges are purposefully planted boundaries. Later, as time went on, hedges took on other functions, including the one we most recognize today: ornament. Built at the height of hedging use in Europe, the sixteenth-century gardens at Hampton Court in London represent the acme of the hedge experience. Hedges were used to make outdoor garden rooms, the famous giant labyrinth, and knot gardens. Hedges became part of entertainment and relaxation for royalty and the wealthy landowners.

Hedges became building-like, creating rooms and walls that were extensions of the internal structures. In the photo at right, the tea house wall is the same line as the hedge, forming a seamless movement from one structure to the other. With doors open, one could be inside out and outside in. The tea house is part of the garden, not just in the garden.

▲ In La Foce Gardens, Val d'Orcia, Italy, there is an amazing view of the countryside. In the background are ancient hedgerows and ravines, and alleés of Italian cypress (*Cupressus sempervirens*) winding up the hillside. The mid-ground of the photo consists of the wall of hedges resembling old castle walls, and in the foreground, you see the tightly clipped severe hedges in geometric forms. The dichotomy between the ancient hedgerows and the hedge made of yew (*Taxus* sp.) shows the power of man's control over nature.

Opposite, bottom: Topiary at Hampton Court Palace

Right: Ladew Topiary Gardens in Monkton, Maryland, was one of the early topiary gardens (1930s) in the United States. Here you can see one of the many hedges that was created at Ladew.

Bottom: The fox hunt, Ladew Topiary Gardens in Monkton, Maryland.

Topiary

Topiary was another art form that sprung up as hedges became muses for the delight of the wealthy. Animals and all sorts of shapes and forms were created from hedges. Boxwood (*Buxus sempervirens*) and yew (*Taxus* spp.) were used to create the giant sculptures.

The shapes that are in the photo at right show the whimsical nature of topiary. In the photo below, the fox hunt is displayed in hedges at Ladew Topiary Gardens in Monkton, Maryland.

There have been many books written about topiary since the first book was written in 1904 by Charles H. Curtis, called *The Book of Topiary*. Up until that time, the only documentation on topiary was mentioned in gardeners' notes throughout Europe. Topiary developed in the early United States as people traveled back and forth to Europe—they learned the techniques on how to clip and construct the large marvels.

Right: Hedge being constructed with the use of pipes at Ladew Topiary Gardens. The internal structures help to support the giant Canadian hemlock (*Tsuga canadensis*) topiary. The trees will be shaped to fit the voids over time. Ladew's gardens were influenced by his travels to France. Like Ladew, many of his contemporaries traveled back and forth to Europe. Other gardens in the US began building topiaries around the same time period.

Below: You can see the large ornate topiary at Longwood Gardens. The main shrub used in these large specimens is Japanese yew (*Taxus cuspidata*), along with several other species of yew.

An exchange of ideas about hedgerows, hedges, topiaries, and other landscaping and gardening trends has gone back and forth between the United States and Europe since colonial times; it continues to this day.

Today, topiary continues to be popular, especially in children's gardens, zoos, and places like Disneyland and Walt Disney World. We see the influence of topiary every day as we drive down main street America and see someone's neatly clipped hedge or round shorn shrub. And we see the influence that topiary has had in the green industry through the development of plants that have more expressive shapes without the help of hedge shears.

Hedges and Their Uses Today

From a design perspective, hedges can be an important structural element of garden design. They create microclimates to provide protection for plants needing a

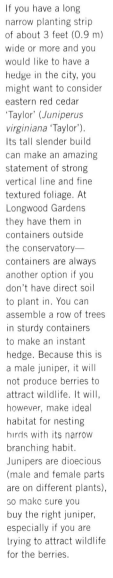

If you have a long narrow planting strip of about 3 feet (0.9 m) wide or more and you would like to have a hedge in the city, you might want to consider eastern red cedar 'Taylor' (*Juniperus virginiana* 'Taylor'). Its tall slender build can make an amazing statement of strong vertical line and fine textured foliage. At Longwood Gardens they have them in containers outside the conservatory— containers are always another option if you don't have direct soil to plant in. You can assemble a row of trees in sturdy containers to make an instant hedge. Because this is a male juniper, it will not produce berries to attract wildlife. It will, however, make ideal habitat for nesting birds with its narrow branching habit. Junipers are dioecious (male and female parts are on different plants), so make sure you buy the right juniper, especially if you are trying to attract wildlife for the berries.

warmer hardiness zone, and they can shield plants that can't handle windy locations.

A new hedge can consist of one species of shrub or small tree, or numerous species to add diversity and depth. You can even try creating a modern hedgerow by planting long strips of various species of shrubs with a tree here and there, adding perennials and annuals to create an environment reminiscent of an ancient hedgerow. These strips of contrived plant groups will eventually form their own plant community that provides valuable habitat, animal corridors, and wind blocks, all while adding a greater depth and dimension to the garden.

Single species hedges can be planted in a straight line, or they can be planted in a zigzag fashion that provides another dimension to the planting. Hedges can also be planted in alternating patterns of mixed shrubs, providing a variation in width and height. Hedges can be used to make garden rooms and are invaluable for adding privacy.

Hedge Idea Gallery

Some of the most interesting plants coming out in today's market are for creating hedges. Hedges have become an important landscaping element to create privacy screens—especially as more people move into our cities. Just because you live in the city doesn't mean you can't get your healthy dose of green every day. City properties may not always have a great deal of space, but they can still lend themselves to a beautiful border hedge. Not only will the hedge provide a lovely backdrop for your garden, it will also add visual texture, color, and line. The hedge can block winds and provide additional wildlife habitat in an area where habitat is usually fragmented or nonexistent.

▲ Another narrow-growing upright plant for hedging is American arborvitae 'American Pillar' (*Thuja occidentalis* 'American Pillar'). The trees can be planted directly in the ground, planted in containers, or, in the case of the photo above, used on a berm to provide privacy and baffle noise along a busy roadway. The hedge can also be a great backdrop for plants of interest on the inside of the garden. The shrubs in the middle of the photo from left to right are flowering quince DOUBLE TAKE ORANGE™ (*Chaenomeles speciosa* 'Orange Storm') and Carolina allspice (*Calycanthus floridus* 'Aphrodite'). In the front is smooth hydrangea INCREDIBALL® BLUSH (*Hydrangea arborescens* 'NCHA4'). Each one of the shrubs can be used to make hedges, but with much different results.

▲ Another option for narrow spaces is American arborvitae (*Thuja occidentalis* 'SMTOTM' Thin Man™). It is slightly wider than 'Taylor' and a completely different texture. The thin columnar form requires little to no maintenance.

▶ If you want something dramatically different that will provide edible fruit, look no further than the cornelian cherry dogwood (*Cornus mas*) hedge that surrounds the rose garden at the Chicago Botanic Garden. Although this hedge requires work, the berries that it produces will certainly be worth the work of pruning. The red berries or drupes have been used for centuries in Europe and Western Asia. It makes a wonderful jam with full-bodied flavor. The fruits are tart—a little sweeter than cranberries or sour cherries—and make a healthful juice. Other benefits of the plant are the small clusters of citrus-colored flowers in the spring and the beautiful fall foliage. Winter interest is excellent too, with its flaking bark.

◀ What about a highbush blueberry (*Vaccinium corymbosum*) hedge? These edible-berried shrubs can be used in the back garden or at the top of the driveway as long as soils are acidic—if not, they can be planted in containers. Blueberries in containers work well to create a privacy screen for the summer months. In the winter, the beautiful green and red stems add winter interest to the landscape. If you are concerned about our pollinator friends—as we all should be—you'll be happy to know that this plant attracts droves of spring pollinators. In the fall an amazing blaze of red foliage will delight the senses. During a visit to Solebury Orchards in New Hope Pennsylvania, the blueberry bushes were inviting with their red glow.

▲ One of the oldest cultivated shrubs in the world is camellia (*Camellia* spp.). It has an ancient connection to tea production, and other species of camellia continue to be desirable for bonsai. While walking in the Old Georgetown section of Washington, D.C., I found this lovely hedge of camellia blooming on Christmas Day. The clean white flowers against the deep green foliage stood out against the whitewashed wall.

◀ Another trimmed hedge that appealed to me was this wonderfully embossed-leaved David viburnum (*Viburnum davidii*). The texture of the leaf is enough for some, but others might enjoy the flowers in the spring and the berries that follow. Its evergreen quality provides a highly sought-after texture for the winter garden. A dioecious plant, you will need male and female specimens for fruiting—certainly worth the effort to find. In northern climates the shrub will be semi-evergreen to deciduous. The hedge in this photo was taken at Kiftsgate Court Gardens, Gloucestershire, England.

▼ Although Ladew Topiary Gardens in Monkton, Maryland, is known for its topiaries, it has a vast diversity in garden design. While visiting a few years ago, I saw this sweetly fragrant wave-like visual of Virginia sweetspire 'Henry's Garnet' (*Itea virginica* 'Henry's Garnet'). The hedge directly behind and the trees off in the distance on a foggy morning set a dimensional quality that you can't get with smaller plants.

▲ It's not often that you see a hedge or a grouping of Chinese redbud 'Don Egolf' (*Cercis chinensis* 'Don Egolf'). The wonderful bloom in the spring jolts the senses into a full spring throttle. The small tree with a large shrub appearance is ideal for making a peek-a-boo hedge. If you would like to add pops of spring color to a large area, plant the Chinese redbud in repeated groupings, and in between the gaps plant upright groupings of evergreens like American arborvitae THIN MAN™. In front of THIN MAN™ and around the bases of the Chinese redbuds, you can plant low shrubs that bloom later in the season, such as smooth hydrangea (*Hydrangea arborescens* INVINCIBELLE Mini Mauvette™). The mauve blooms will echo the early pink Chinese redbud blooms and will last the entire summer. Then the smooth hydrangea heads will provide winter interest along the border.

◀ Smooth hydrangea INVINCIBELLE Mini Mauvette™ also makes a wonderful blooming hedge by itself.

▶ Wintertime is just as important as spring, summer, and fall. This picture shows how shrubs pique visual interest in the landscape along the longwalk at Longwood Gardens. American arborvitae (*Thuja occidentalis* 'Nigra') and yellow twig dogwood (*Cornus sericea* 'Flaviramea') coexist with numerous other evergreen shrubs. The yellow twig dogwood canes offer vibrant color for winter interest. They will be cut each spring, with the oldest canes removed down to the ground. Yellow twig dogwood is a wonderful plant for wet sites, where it provides great stabilizing effects for soil with its fibrous root system.

◀ Rhododendrons are magnificent plants and are wonderful for rich, deep, moist, acidic soils and rarely need pruning. They like the cooler latitudes and in some areas are losing ground due to climate change. Through the Appalachian Mountains and up through New England they grow with ease, escaping most of the hot summer nights. Ideally, they prefer partial shade to protect them from the scorching summer sun. They will flower more profusely in full sun with adequate moisture, but the flowers usually don't last as long as those planted in the shade. Azaleas are included in the rhododendron genus, but they are one of eight subgroups within the genus. Rhododendrons have ten stamens while azaleas have five—a great ID feature. There are some hybrid crosses that have seven stamens. For the most part, rhododendrons are evergreen, with leaves ranging from tiny to extra-large. In the photo to the left, you will see rhododendron (*Rhododendron* 'Alice Poore') as an under-canopy hedge. The massive blooms at the end of May and beginning of June fill a flower void until other plants are blooming. Hay-scented fern (*Dennstaedtia punctilobula*) in bright green provides a nice contrast in texture.

▶ On a recent visit to a plant breeder's home, I was greeted along the drive by this amazing hedge of smooth hydrangea INCREDIBALL® (*Hydrangea arborescens* 'Abetwo' INCREDIBALL®). It was a take-your-breath-away moment. INCREDIBALL® is an improved 'Annabelle' that has thicker stems to hold up the enormous heads that rise just above the foliage. Every year the plant will put on the same show because the giant blooms occur on new wood. The flowers start out green, transitioning to a pure white. They hold up well as a cut flower. The flower heads remain on the plant all winter, adding another season of interest. Spent flower heads can be removed in spring by pruning the entire plant to 6 inches (15 cm) above the ground. Smooth hydrangea loves moist soil—if you have an area on your property that receives runoff, this is an ideal location for INCREDIBALL®.

▼ A massive hedge of catawba rhododendron (*Rhododendron catawbiense*) protects the entrance to the Sullivan Renaissance building in Liberty, New York.

Salt-Tolerant Hedges and Shrubs for Low-Lying Areas

Hedges planted in low-lying areas can protect vulnerable soil and provide stability to prevent washouts. Salt-tolerant species are ideal planted along roadways or on beach properties. The next time that you are along the coast, notice what is growing well in the environment. This will provide a huge hint as to what to plant along roadways and sidewalks to withstand winter road salt applications in colder climates. Planted along the marsh in the photo below is bayberry (*Myrica pensylvanica*). Bayberry is a versatile plant that makes a phenomenal hedge anywhere there happens to be high salt spray. Even without salt spray, this plant does beautifully in partially shaded areas along a woodland edge, in a city setting, or in full sun. Groundsel bush (*Baccharis halimifolia*) is typically found in the eastern part of the United States along the coast and inland coastal wetlands. It has a high salt tolerance and can be rare in some locations. The fall bloom is amazing—being in the aster family (Asteraceae), it blooms in white fluffy masses, and the seed disperses through the air. The leaves are small and semi-evergreen to deciduous.

Native peoples have a close association to Eastern red cedar (*Juniperus virginiana*), using it for medicinal purposes. The thin branches and berries were used in preparing deer meat and making tea. The tree comes in many forms, many of which are shrubs. They are extremely salt tolerant and have rot-resistant wood.

Salt-tolerant species—Beach Plum Island State Park, Delaware

Don't forget low hedges that can provide a multitude of services—for pollinators, for medicinals, and for softening the harsh lines of a walkway. In the fields at Snow Hill Lavender Farm in Broadway, England, the subshrub of English lavender (*Lavandula angustifolia* cv.) is planted out in rows reminiscent of old farm fields. The ancient hedgerows are in the distance.

How to Prune a Hedge

Pruning hedges can be a joyous job or a laborious one, depending on how you view the activity. In the diagrams below, you will see two forms of hedging—one that is looser in structure and one that is more defined and formal in nature. Each has its own unique way of being pruned to yield the desired outcome.

When pruning a more casual or soft hedge (Figure A), pruning cuts will be made in several locations. The first pruning cuts are located at the base of the plant to remove the oldest of the canes. Removing canes does not affect the overall shape of the hedge, it just reduces the overall height and sometimes the width of the shrub. Basically, you're performing selective thinning as described in Chapter 6. These cuts could also be considered reduction cuts, because you are reducing the overall size of the shrub when removing the oldest canes. If the shrub is deciduous, it is best to do this in the winter so you can visually see the shape of the shrub without leaves. If it is a spring bloomer, you can still prune in this fashion, but if you are sending the cut stems to market, make sure there is significant color in the buds before pruning.

If the shrub is too far gone and really needs rejuvenation, you can also stool the plant (see Chapter 6) or reduce the plant to a few main stems. Once the plant is reduced dramatically, a two-year pruning cycle should be carried out as mentioned above.

With pruning heavily shorn hedges, as in boxed hedges (Figure B), a different approach is taken. If the shrub is too tall and wide, shearing may have to be done directly before the new growth emerges

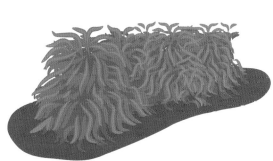

FIGURE A

FIGURE B

▲ At Morton Arboretum in Lisle, Illinois, there is a wonderful area that displays different types of hedges. They also exhibit different ways in which the hedges can be pruned. Visiting an arboretum or botanic garden can inspire ideas of what to use in your own garden, especially when there are examples of hedges and trimming techniques on display.

◀ Windows are cut in the hedges and topiaries to increase air flow at Longwood Gardens in Kennett Square, Pennsylvania.

and then again afterward. You may need to take the shrub back several inches (cm) to keep its size in check. The following year it can be reduced even further in the same manner. This type of pruning is called heading back (see Chapter 6) and should only be done on shrubs if you are hedging them and you want the close-shorn look. It should not be done on street trees or other large trees or shrubs.

You will note that there are darker patches on the hedge in Figure B. These are purposeful windows cut into the hedge to allow for air movement. The cuts are made with pruners to take out a branch without opening too much of a hole. This technique is used at Longwood Gardens on their hedges and topiaries to reduce insect problems and disease and provide plenty of air movement.

You will also notice that the hedge in Figure B has a pyramid-like shape, with a wider bottom and a narrower top. This ensures that there is enough light to penetrate the interior of the shrub. The technique also encourages better airflow.

CHAPTER 9

ATTRACTING POLLINATORS AND OTHER DESIRABLE WILDLIFE

Planting an array of plants that attract wildlife will undoubtedly benefit the overall environment and our animal communities. Through compassionate attention to "the other," we are also helping ourselves. We have evolved and learned from our animal counterparts by building our apartment houses like beehives and living in cell-like structures. Modern homes are comparable to a groundhog's burrow, with several escape routes, including front, back, and side doors. We even "swarm around" when we're worried, just like bees when they lose their queen. Our roads are built to follow the early paths of deer movement, and we have constructed our highways to mimic the super flyways of bird migration heading north and south.

Understanding the threat of species loss can help us build diverse and resilient ecosystems, increasing plant community relationships with animals and ourselves. Finding a balance within the landscape can help prevent ecosystem collapse, which is usually followed by species extinction. In the article "Home Gardens in the Maintenance of Biological Diversity," Mary Agbogidi and E.B. Adolor talk about the importance of diversity. "Home gardens take on the character of the surrounding ecological system and provide a place where plants, animals, insects, micro-organisms and soil and air media mutually interact. . ." By creating these environments, we learn to observe what comes in and out of our gardens, and if we are diligent enough, we take written notes on our observations. Citizen science is the result of our observations and documentation. Over time, observations help us to make informed decisions for plant selection while designing gardens for enjoyment and relaxation.

Getting Children Involved

Animal activity in the garden should bring enjoyment to all ages. Children who keep track of the number and types of birds and other animals coming into the garden are provided a new level of educational action and awareness. A large chalkboard or special book for drawing, taking notes, and taking photos can be the foci of the

Bottlebrush buckeye (*Aesculus parviflora*), Wyck Historic House, Garden, and Farm, Philadelphia, Pennsylvania

activities. Having a few good bird books for identification is helpful too! These activities help children (as well as adults) recognize that we are part of the landscape, interacting with the very animals that we observe. Gardening is not just planting plants, but understanding the larger context of the interaction of the garden with the surrounding community, locally and globally.

Why is it important for us to have habitat in our backyards for animals? As our world becomes more developed, the open spaces that animals once had to roam and graze are smaller. The disruption of their habitat can be circumvented by conscious homeowners willing to replace what has been lost.

Diversity Becomes Key

In all cases, we know that animals (including humans) and plants are intricately connected across the globe. We are dependent on each other for our survival. Understanding these connections enables us to be conscious of our actions in our gardens, making pleasing landscapes while providing a multitude of amenities for other creatures. If plants are selected carefully, native and non-native plants can cohabitate and provide many benefits for the ecosystem.

What Do Animals Do in Our Environment?

Insects, bats, numerous bird species, and wind all help to pollinate our plants. Providing opportunities for pollination also

The juvenile ruby-throated hummingbird (*Archilochus colubris*) is attracted to tubular-shaped flowers like those of the red buckeye (opposite page).

leads to the production of fruits for later animal activity and our consumption.

Animals like deer help certain plants to sprout from the roots through their hoof movements. Squirrels help to disperse seed to new areas of the landscape as they hide their winter store, a task that typically goes unnoticed by our eyes. Birds also help to disperse seed through their droppings, helping entire new plant communities to spring up where there was once an old field or empty lot. Even the fur and paws of wolf, coyote, and fox carry valuable seed to new locations. Don't undervalue our animal friends and the work they do for our own benefit. It would be remiss if we did. Providing birds with habitat for quiet respites during migration, as well as places for nesting, are other ways that we can help. Understanding animal movement will certainly lead to better selections of shrubs for our landscapes while beautifying our personal spaces.

Interconnectivity

Insects and birds are attracted to numerous characteristics of plants, including fragrance, elevation, texture, shape and form, color, line, lighting, and other complex patterns within the landscape. These intricate patterns only occur through diversity within the landscape.

We talked about ID features in Chapter 3, and each of the identification features translates into a visual form of communication to insects and birds. Opposite, alternate, and whorled leaf configurations create different matrices that allow animals to move quickly or slowly in their shadows. A mix of deciduous and evergreen shrubs and trees provides an additional form of

protection at different seasons and times of day. Planting your garden with a variety of flower sizes, shapes, colors, and floral patterns—in addition to different directional approaches—will appeal to a vast array of pollinators.

Remember that how we see the garden is not how pollinators see it. If we try to create a varied landscape, we create the smorgasbord that insects and birds are looking for. A drone flying over the garden can give a better hint of the matrices that insects and birds see from above the garden.

The Value of Diverse Bloom Times

Bloom cycles of plants are correlated with bird and insect movement. Red buckeye (*Aesculus pavia*) is a good example of a plant that has timed its bloom with the return of hummingbirds after a long winter. When red buckeye is in bloom, hummingbirds are sure to be close by, along with butterflies and other pollinators.

Below, left: An American robin (*Turdus migratorius*) sits in the branches of an American holly while eating the berries at his early spring northern destination.

Below, right: Seedlings of the American holly sprouting after being deposited in bird droppings at the base of an eastern white pine tree (*Pinus strobus*)

As climate change continues, we will see modifications in migration. Many plant species are shifting to the north (called "plant creep") due to temperature increases. Red buckeye is a good example of one plant that is adapting to more northern climes. Once only found in southern states, it now can be found in the Mid-Atlantic and Midwest regions, providing valuable pollinator services. In most cases, plants with large seeds like red buckeye are moved by larger animals, including humans.

Pollinators

Keeping bees is a wonderful way to make the connection between pollinators and flowers. Beekeepers tend to have more plants in their gardens to feed their pollinators, making sure that there is something in bloom almost year-round.

Native, solitary bee species (of which there are nearly 4,000 in North America alone!) are equally important when it comes to pollination, along with beetles, wasps, flies, and butterflies.

Late winter and early spring are important times for pollinators, especially the first warm days of the season. The first blooms to burst with color and fragrance attract hungry insects to pollinate their fresh blooms. Watching insects carrying pollen grains from one flower to another assures us that pollination is happening and there will be an ample fruit set.

A great activity for children is to count and photograph as many pollinators as possible. Having a book on insects is a handy tool for them to use, especially if they're not using cell phones.

Poop Is Important

Numerous species of shrubs and other plants are reliant on seed dispersal by birds carrying seed in their droppings. In this case, the seed must pass through the gut of the bird in order to germinate.

The acid from the birds' stomachs scarifies (removes a thick coating) the seed before it's deposited on fertile ground to grow. American holly (*Ilex opaca*) is a wonderful example of a plant with an avian partnership. Although the seed is not totally reliant on birds, the process through a bird's gut makes the process more efficient. On the East Coast where American holly is abundant, seedlings sprout readily from the avian and plant partnership. Migration disperses the seed out of the local area, which diversifies the genetic pool of the American holly while extending its range.

Migration

Migratory routes are closely linked to wetland sites, and when we talk about wetlands, ponds, and rain gardens in Chapter 10, we'll discuss additional plants that are in migratory areas.

Birds are much like humans in that they have certain foods that most of them enjoy eating while traveling. There are general foods that are spread over large areas, and then there are regional foods that are unique to a specific site. Birds benefit from these regional nuances when they are nesting or overwintering. A plant that has a smaller range compared to other food sources may have specific nutrients for nesting birds or a higher fat content to keep birds warm over winter. Even a certain instar of an insect that's found in a region on specific plants can be a critical food source for baby bird development, or it could be a trigger for migration. The network of interconnectivity between the bird, insect, and plant world goes far beyond our human comprehension at present.

Migration Flyways

According to BirdLife International, there are eight major migratory flyways worldwide. There are many lesser migratory flyways with shorter migratory distances, but they are by no means less important. In the United States, we have three major flyways that cross through our airspace and one shorter one, according to Audubon. The latter runs through the Mississippi River region.

The major flyways generally take a north-south flight pattern that constitutes thousands of miles of migration by an enormous population of bird species. To maintain their energy for long flights, birds need fat- and protein-rich food sources each time they touch down to rest. Those of us living near major flyways can help our avian friends by filling our gardens with native shrubs that provide ready food sources and places to hide from predators.

The flyway regions are not strictly for birds—insects use them too! On the ground, these regions are where other animal species travel and seek food and habitat. Even human populations have selectively developed our dense population centers in and along flyways.

Over millennia, plant-animal associations have strengthened and evolved into a complex network of mutual dependence. We have seen this scenario play out most recently with monarch butterflies and milkweed (*Asclepias* spp.). These butterflies rely exclusively on milkweed for survival, and the decline in milkweed populations due to habitat loss has, in part, caused a decline in monarchs.

Black chokeberry (*Aronia melanocarpa*) grows along the coast of New England

Atlantic Americas Flyway—For the Birds and Others

The Atlantic Americas Flyway comprises an area from the northern reaches of Canada to southern South America. The pathway is defined by a slightly S-shaped pattern on a global map, which at times hugs the Atlantic coastline of the United States and continues to hug the coastline of the entire length of South America. The USDA website (https://plants.usda.gov/java/) is excellent for researching which bird-friendly plants to consider for your landscape. When using this resource, enter a plant name, then select the plant—the first page will give a plant locator map depicting the ranges for the plant. If the plant is native to the United States, the color of the

information will be in green, and if the plant is non-native, the color will be blue, indicating the spread of the plant in various regions throughout the country.

If you don't know nativity and plant range information before purchasing plants, these maps become an invaluable tool. Certain shrub species such as red chokeberry (*Aronia arbutifolia*) can be seen growing along the east coast on the map, mirroring the Atlantic Americas Flyway, and it's not by accident. Red chokeberry has a long association with birds that travel this route. The shrub also feeds local populations of birds that don't migrate. In the spring, the shrub blooms in white clusters of flowers with lavender/plum anthers, attracting pollinators from far and wide. There are numerous cultivars that are excellent for planting in your garden for greater diversity. The showiest of the cultivars is red chokeberry 'Brilliantissima,' with its fire-engine-red, shiny fall foliage and screaming red berries that typically stay on over the winter. These berries are eaten by bird species that return in late winter when the berries are at peak ripeness. For us, the shrub's red fall color is an added visual benefit before the cold winter sets in.

The red chokeberry fruits are so bright red they can be seen from the air—a calling card for hungry migrating birds.

and the Mid-Atlantic states before it turns inland to the Midwest, continuing down the Appalachian Mountains to Georgia, according to USDA maps. The shrub can be found growing in mountainous wetlands as well as along inland coastal areas. The deep-colored berries are high in antioxidants and are a rich food source for birds, other animals, and humans. The plant was taken to Europe at some point during human migration, and in the early twentieth century it became popular in northern and eastern Europe, as well as in Russia. It is grown extensively in Poland to make nutritious juices, jams, and jellies.

Besides being an excellent food source, the black chokeberry plant has amazing yellow and orange fall color that adds to the landscape's visual beauty.

Swamp titi (*Cyrilla racemiflora*) inhabits an enormous range of wetland habitat—from Delaware to Florida and west to Texas and then through the Caribbean and down along the eastern coast of South America. It is cold tolerant in some protected northern ranges even though it is a southern species. The only drawback in colder climates—it may lose its semi-evergreen leaves during colder winters.

In South America, swamp titi is a taller variation of the species found in the United States. All along the Atlantic Americas Flyway, swamp titi acts as good protection for birds while supplying small-beaked birds with tiny seeds to eat. Watching pollinator activity on swamp titi is mesmerizing. A myriad of insects pollinate the sweet, small, nectarous flowers, producing a highly prized honey.

Swamp titi has a close association with white-tailed deer. Deer like to browse this plant, and when they move around the plant, their hooves encourage the roots to sprout, eventually forming massive thickets. In northern areas the white-tailed deer don't eat it, and the plant doesn't sprout from the roots like in the southern states. The plants in the north are typically solitary.

Negative Consequences during Food Shortages

During food shortages—which can occur because of bitterly cold temperatures, extreme drought, a small crop season, or habitat loss—birds may be forced to eat foods that they typically don't eat. For them, it is a huge risk to eat something that is not in their memory store. If it turns out to be a good food source, they may eat it again if necessary or begin including it in their regular diet. But if it turns out the food source is not healthy for them, they may die. In a recent case in Georgia, a flock of cedar waxwings was found dead. When an autopsy was completed by the College of Veterinary Medicine at the University of Georgia, they found the birds died from a high number of nandina (*Nandina domestica*) berries in their stomachs. This was not a typical food source for the waxwings, and the veterinarians believe that cyanide found in the berries was the culprit. Nandina berries are not typically toxic to humans, but can be lethal to birds, cats, and grazing animals. To prevent animal poisoning, consider other options or remove the berries when they develop.

Right: Eastern red cedar 'Blue Mountain' NORDIC® exhibits wonderful blue foliage in a spreading form. It works great on slopes and in areas that could use a barrier. Salt tolerant, this plant does well along salty roadways The berries (cones) are highly desirable to birds.

Below: Winterberry 'Maryland Beauty' produces more berries than many of the variations within the species—and it has a beautiful overall stature.

Other Plants along the Atlantic Americas Flyway

Winterberry (*Ilex verticillata*) has a huge variation within the species. Bloom times can be several weeks apart depending on which part of the country they're growing in. The wide range of bloom times ensures that there will be plenty of food for birds and other small mammals to garner. The variation within the species of this plant is where many of our new cultivars come from. Plants that exhibit higher berry count, longer-lasting berries, and desirable overall form are named and put into cultivation in the nursery trade. Winterberry 'Maryland Beauty' is one variety that was selected for its profusion of berries, providing a plentiful food supply while offering up amazing brilliant red fruits. The berry stems are excellent for cut flower use as an added bonus.

Eastern red cedar (*Juniperus virginiana*) is a conifer inhabiting the Atlantic shoreline. It's also found in the Central Americas

Flyway and the Mississippi Flyway (mentioned on page 178). Eastern red cedar feeds an enormous array of animals while creating invaluable habitat. There are huge numbers of variations within the species, including spreaders, tall and narrow upright forms, and pyramid-shaped forms. The color of the foliage can vary greatly. Depending on your landscape preference, you can purchase dark greens, blue greens, bright greens, and chartreuse forms.

Right: Smooth hydrangea (*Hydrangea arborescens* ssp. *radiata*) is a lacecap flower form of smooth hydrangea with sterile flowers surrounding fertile flowers in the center. The prolific blooms are fragrant and attract beetles, bees, and butterflies.

Below: Smooth hydrangea is an ideal plant for the garden, attracting pollinators and small birds. It blooms consistently each year because it blooms on new wood. Flower heads make a good cut flower.

Central Americas Flyway and the Mississippi Flyway

The Central Americas Flyway starts in the vast open space of central Canada and continues down into the central United States through the Great Plains. It parallels the Mississippi Flyway, eventually merging with parts of it before heading down through Texas. It then heads over the Gulf of Mexico and into parts of Central America and central South America.

Smooth hydrangea (*Hydrangea arborescens*) is one of many plants found in the Midwest that is ideal for pollinators, while their tiny seeds are delectable for smaller birds. The plants' height can reach 10 feet (3 m) in some isolated cases, according to

the Missouri Botanical Garden. Smooth hydrangea has consistently large bloom heads grown on new wood, assuring animals a dependable food supply. Planting this shrub in deep, rich, moist soil will ensure a phenomenal display in the garden, all while feeding hungry insects and birds.

Smooth hydrangea grows in the Atlantic Americas Flyway too, making the shrub an important food source for vast populations of birds and insects. If you love this plant, there are new varieties of smooth hydrangea being released frequently. (See Chapter 5 for additional information.)

Another plant that can be found along the Central Americas and Mississippi Flyways is the American cranberrybush (*Viburnum opulus* var. *americanum*). It's typically found in the upper tier of the United States from the West Coast to the East Coast and up through Canada. The fruits resemble cranberries (*Vaccinium macrocarpon*) and are edible—jams and jellies can be made from the fruit. Birds love the fruits, and butterflies and other pollinators love the flat-topped flowers (cymes) that bloom in the spring. There is also a yellow-berried form that is equally beautiful, and each form has wonderful fall foliage that varies in color from yellow to orange and rose to wine.

Spicebush (*Lindera benzoin*) is an extremely important plant found along the Atlantic Americas, Central Americas, and Mississippi Flyways. Having a wide growing range means spicebush can feed a diverse population of animals. As the days begin to warm in the spring, spicebush

Left: Oregon grapeholly (*Mahonia aquifolium*) not only services bird populations, it also serves humans. A tart grape-like juice, jelly, and wine can be made from the berries. A yellow dye is made from the stems of the plant.

Right: Plant California lilac for its seeds and flowers to attract butterflies, birds, and other wildlife. The seed in the photo is from an unknown species in the Los Angeles area.

is an early bloomer attracting small bees and flies. Fourteen different bird species have been seen eating the berries on the female plants in the fall, including robins, wood thrushes, catbirds, and veeries. Deer sometimes nibble this plant but typically prefer other delicacies. The shrub grows in the understory in woodlands, in some cases growing as far as the eye can see. Riparian areas also contain vast expanses of the plant, which has a yellow-gold fall color. Spice-bush likes moist soils with high organic content. The shrub can be grown in the garden setting in partially sunny areas with drier soils, but the plant won't get as large as in moist soils. According to Lucy Meriwether Lewis Marks's writings, the plant's leaves can be used as an insect repellent.

Pacific Americas Flyway

The third major flyway begins in Alaska and hugs the coastline of the western United States through Central America before continuing down the western coast of South America. Plant communities are key for the success of any migratory movement

along the trail. On the West Coast, Oregon grapeholly (*Mahonia aquifolium*) follows the coastline from Alaska through Canada to Southern California. The berries and flowers provide food for countless birds and opportunities galore for pollinators. Some pollinators and other insects migrate like birds and benefit from having ready food sources along the way.

California lilac (*Ceanothus* spp.) is found in the Pacific Americas Flyway and throughout the lower forty-eight states and Canada. In other parts of the country, the common name changes according to the species and its uses. There are sixty-four different species of *Ceanothus* found in the United States that accommodate a plethora of birds and insects. The species' ranges can be found on the USDA website under the Latin genus name. The flower color of the shrub can range from white to deep blue, lavender, and soft pink. California lilac 'Marie Simon' (*Ceanothus* × *pallidus* 'Marie Simon') has soft pink flowers.

Like its California counterpart, New Jersey tea (*Ceanothus americanus*) is

Left: New Jersey tea can range in color from white to pale blue. Its blooms and foliage attract over forty species for pollination and grazing.

Right: There are many species of serviceberry throughout the United States. Alder-leaved serviceberry is found in all the flyways in the United States. 'Pembina' is a cultivar that was selected for its large berries.

important, crossing the Central Americas Flyway, the Mississippi Flyway, and the Atlantic Americas Flyway. New Jersey tea, also known as redroot, can be found on the eastern side of the Continental Divide. Used for a tea substitute during the American Revolution, its anti-microbial elements helped in ailments of the mouth and to speed blood coagulation. Hosting over forty different animal species, *Ceanothus* is very important across the United States and even into Canada.

The alder-leaved serviceberry (*Amelanchier alnifolia*) encompasses a huge area along the Pacific Americas Flyway—from the far reaches of Alaska along the Canadian coast and down to the tip of Southern California. The shrub also inhabits the upper tiers of the Central and Atlantic Americas Flyways into the deep interior of Canada. The shrub or small tree produces a profusion of berries after its floral display of white flowers in spring. Alder-leaved serviceberry lives up to its name by servicing huge populations of birds and other animals, including humans. It suckers from its roots, so even if it's grazed it will pop back up to continue its mission of servicing the masses. Planting a hedgerow of alder-leaved serviceberry will not only provide a beautiful white bloom in spring and berries for everyone, the fall color will complete the growing season in yellow, orange, and red tones.

CHAPTER 10

SHRUBS FOR PONDS, CREEKS, RAIN GARDENS, HILLSIDES, AND RIPARIAN AREAS

Before we talk about water-related landscape features, we need to discuss water in general—how it moves through our landscapes and how that movement can be influenced by shrubs. As a horticulturist and designer, it is difficult for me not to talk about environments surrounding our own properties, because land does not sit disconnected from the larger environment. In order to make the right plant selections for gardens, we need to understand plants and their functions. Utilizing a plant's ability is just as important as the beauty they provide and the food that they may contribute to all animals, including humans.

Plants selected for water corridors and water retention sites should have fibrous or massive root systems in order to hold back tons of soil and silt. This will prevent erosion and contribute to water retention and stabilization. Shrubs provide cooling and consistent temperatures in the heat of the summer along streambanks and other bodies of water, which benefits animals and the entire ecosystem.

Many shrubs have the ability to quickly asexually reproduce using three primary strategies.

- The first strategy: develop new shoots off the root system to form entire colonies of multi-stemmed shrubs
- The second strategy: fallen branches and entire limbs adventitiously root along their surface where they touch the ground
- The third strategy: natural layering when shrub stems bend down, touch the ground, and take root while still attached to the mother plant (see Chapter 7 for how to "force" this process.)

These strategies are key to mitigating water issues in the landscape.

Beachside Plant Communities

Another example of shrubs and their strategies is the successional growth along coastlines, where sand is shifted by the action of waves and wind. Go slightly inland after the established grassy dunes of American

Common witch hazel (*Hamamelis virginiana*) blooms along streambanks October through December, providing a sweet and medicinal fragrance.

Above: Beach plum (*Prunus maritima*) found in the beach border helps to stabilize dunes and deposit leaf litter for later successional growth. The shrub is important for bird migration, pollinators, and rabbits, and it provides a luscious fruit for jams and jellies. Beach plum can be planted along salty roadways to expand animal habitat.

Right, top: Purple-flowering raspberry (*Rubus odoratus*) roots itself firmly in the rock and gravel escarpment in Ithaca, New York.

Right, bottom: Purple-flowering raspberry (*Rubus odoratus*)

beachgrass (*Ammophila breviligulata*), with its deep root system, and you will find the shrubby border that includes other perennial plants like mullein (*Verbascum* spp.) and Virginia creeper (*Parthenocissus quinquefolia*).

This shrubby border stabilizes its own community—the second succession after dune grasses and before larger tree growth. The intricate structure of the roots and shrub branches generates a network of associations below and above ground.

Shrubs help to establish the first layers of leaf litter, creating thin layers of organic material that will eventually be broken down and used for nutrients by larger trees and shrubs inland.

The first salt-tolerant shrub community has the tenacity to endure long periods of drought, inundation from fresh and brackish water, cold winter winds, and hurricanes. These durable traits are the very characteristics we look for when establishing plant communities along salty roadways, in ditches, on steep slopes, and along creeks.

Inland Waterways and Their Plant Communities

Freshwater inland shrub communities have a tenacity similar to their coastal shrub counterparts, but they are typically not salt tolerant. They can be seen growing out of rocky outcroppings, steep gravelly slopes, and nutrient-poor soils.

The inland shrub communities are also able to withstand freezing temperatures, extreme heat, and huge swings in water availability, soil pH, soil depth, and lighting.

Additionally, there are many other specific inland shrub communities, but they

are not as adaptable to extremes. A good example is a bog plant community that relies on low soil pH and a specific height to the water table in order to survive. The plants here are not generalists like in the previous two communities discussed, but are specialists within their communities. Plants that grow in high pH soils are another group of specialists that have limited locations for growth. Specialists can grow in our gardens but are usually used in containers, where the soil, pH, and water requirements can be adjusted for the specificity of the plant (e.g., bog gardens).

For the most part, generalists can be found in a wider range of areas throughout the United States. They are typically more adaptable to varying sites, which makes them ideal for our gardens. They can be real workhorses.

When we talk about heavy rain episodes, flooding, and fast-moving water, we can turn to the generalist shrubs—incorporating them into sound designs can stabilize areas that are on the brink of collapse due to erosion.

Watersheds

Major rain episodes can create havoc, but shrubs and other plants can mitigate damage from these events by holding soil in place and buffering the impact of hard rain. If your home is located at the headwaters of a watershed, it's even more important to plant your property and surrounding properties with the utmost care to prevent downstream flooding. Your property's layout and its water resources can change how water flows downstream. If everyone planted streambanks and hillsides with the proper vegetation, there would be less flooding and runoff, leading to cleaner waterways and preserving and increasing wildlife habitat. Municipalities in the United States are required to meet the guidelines of MS4 standards (Municipal Separate Storm Sewer System) from the Amended Clean Water Act of 1987. If residents were aware of the overall cost of storm-water damage to municipalities, they might think more critically about the beneficial impact of plantings on their property. The multiplied effect of these

Right: Planting trees and shrubs that thrive in wet soils—such as this sweetbay magnolia (*Magnolia virginiana*)—reduces both the amount of runoff and the speed at which water moves.

Below: Shrubs, small trees, and spring bulbs are planted on the hillside to prevent erosion and avoid mowing. Photo taken at Winterthur Museum, Garden, and Library, Winterthur, Delaware.

types of plantings across many properties helps enormously during heavy rain events, especially in flood-prone areas.

The most vulnerable areas on your property are hillsides. Planting steep inclines with shrubs reduces overall soil loss and stabilizes the area while reducing the workload for the homeowner. Mowing should not be done on steep hillsides. Shrubs have an amazing capacity to limit the loss of soil when planted in the right area. They also look great and provide cooling effects along sloped streambanks and

other bodies of water. With the increase in major rain events in several regions of the world, think about looking upstream to see how green infrastructure can be reinforced to reduce the speed at which water moves through the watershed. If everyone in a watershed was conscious of this and began looking at their own properties first, even simple measures—such as a reduction in impermeable surfaces and the proper placement of more shrubs—could significantly reduce the amount of runoff.

Surveying Your Property

As a gardener, you can build more resilient gardens and healthier environments around you by paying attention to every inch of your property. During a heavy rainstorm, walk your garden to watch how the water moves through your property. Identify the most vulnerable areas. Draw a simple map showing downspouts and their runoff,

Above: Using partial stone walls, the massive slope is now divided into areas using small shrubs and perennials. This creates microclimates while preventing erosion downhill. Photo taken at Surreybrooke Nursery, Middletown, Maryland.

Rght: Yellowroot has beautiful amethyst-colored, glass-like flowers with a wonderful clean green foliage in the summer. In the fall it turns to a yellow to peach to mauve to maroon.

locate areas that puddle, and note areas that show erosion. Document the areas that are stable and unchanged during the rainstorm. From your observations, you will have a visual map that shows where you need to concentrate your resources first. Heavily eroded areas benefit from massive plantings of shrubs, perennials, and trees. From your diagram, you may even notice ideal spots for building rain gardens, ponds, and other water features.

Positive Actions

DON'T MOW STEEP SLOPES

Mowing steep slopes should be avoided; there are few exceptions. Using no-mow grass and planting shrubs strategically on a slope helps reduce water flow, while at the same time providing varying seasons of interest from the shrubs' bloom to fruit.

USE NATURAL MATERIALS TO ALTER WATER FLOW

Utilizing large fallen logs, boulders, or partial rock walls with shrubs planted on the upside of them works wonders for retarding water. It also allows plant groupings

or garden islands to establish. The newly planted shrubs will add a greater visual diversity to the garden slope while creating additional habitat.

ADD THE RIGHT PLANTS

You can begin by adding plants in stages or as your budget permits. Native plants work best, but that certainly doesn't mean that you can't use other plants that are non-native, non-invasive, and equally tough to handle similar conditions.

Pick varying-sized plants and create small plant communities. Be sure to allow enough room for smaller plants to grow to their full potential. Subshrubs can be planted to fill in the gaps, hugging the ground and adding additional layers for water to be bound. Yellowroot (*Xanthorhiza simplicissima*) or sweet box (*Sarcococca hookeriana* var. *humilis*) create excellent cover. They asexually propagate themselves from

Right: Soil stabilization is achieved by planting red twig dogwood in the riparian area where the stream meets the low bank.

Below: Sweet box is an evergreen groundcover with a shiny deep-green leaf. The late-winter bloom fills the air with a sweet fresh fragrance that attracts pollinators from miles around.

their roots, adding another dimension to the planting. The layering effect of various species of shrubs has the result of a huge net collecting rainwater. Leaf surfaces, stems, and bark all have the potential to hold additional water, creating a giant rain sink on the plants' surfaces. The slow dripping of water from the plants long after a heavy rain is testament to the shrubs' capacity to hold water above ground as well as below.

SHORE UP STREAMBANKS

Along streambanks where there is scouring or deep cuts in the streambank, living logs of willow can be made and secured using rebar. Or cribs can be built on-site and then planted behind to shore up the streambank. Be sure to check with local officials when constructing anything in stream beds. There may be restrictions on what you can and can't do, or there may be grants and other organizational support to help with your streambank restoration project.

Low-lying areas benefit from shrub plantings too! Gradual grades planted with

Bayberry (*Myrica pensylvanica*) stabilizes sand dunes on beaches with standing salt spray, heavy winds, and saltwater inundation. It does equally well along highways and inland streams. Ocean City, New Jersey.

shrubs and perennials will handle inundation and will typically stay intact, holding on to valuable topsoil.

PICK THE RIGHT SHRUBS

What types of plants are ideal for water management and soil stabilization? Typically, plants native to wetlands and riparian corridors (stream or river banks) are the best fit. Some important characteristics of these plants are: quick growth; a deep and fibrous root system; a multi-stemmed structure; and the ability to quickly reproduce by asexual means, such as suckering, layering, off-shoots, and adventitious rooting. The chart on the following pages introduces twenty-three shrubs with these characteristics. It shares information about their size, preferred growing conditions, and flowering time, along with their winter hardiness and a few notable characteristics.

RIPARIAN AND WETLAND SPECIES COMMON NAME	LATIN NAME	TEMPERATURE	OVERALL SIZE HEIGHT X WIDTH	LIGHTING	BLOOM TIME
American black elderberry	Sambucus canadensis	-40°F/-40°C	5'–12' x 5'–12' (1.5–3.6 m x 1.5–3.6 m)	Partial Sun–Full Sun	June–July
Arrowwood viburnum	Viburnum dentatum	-50°F/-46°C	6'–10' x 6'–10' (1.8–3 m x 1.8–3 m)	Full Sun–Partial Shade	May–June
Bayberry	Myrica pensylvanica (Morella)	-30°F/-34°C	5'–10' x 5'–10' (1.5–3 m x 1.5–3 m)	Full Sun–Partial Shade	May
Beach plum	Prunus maritima	-30°F/-34°C	3'–6' x 4'–6' (0.9–1.8 m x 1.2–1.8 m)	Full Sun	April–May
Black chokeberry	Aronia melanocarpa	-40°F/-40°C	3'–6' x 3'–6' (0.9–1.8 m x 0.9–1.8 m)	Full Sun–Partial Shade	May
Bottlebrush buckeye	Aesculus parviflora	-30°F/-34°C	8'–12' x 8'–15' (2.4–3.6 m x 2.4–4.5 m)	Partial Sun–Full Sun	June–July
Buttonbush	Cephalanthus occidentalis	-20°F/-29°C	5'–12' x 4'–8' (1.5–3.6 m x 1.2–2.4 m)	Full Sun–Partial Shade	June
Carolina allspice	Calycanthus floridus	-30°F/-34°C	6'–10' x 6'–12' (1.8–3 m x 1.8–3.6 m)	Full Sun–Partial Shade	April–July
Common witch hazel	Hamamelis virginiana	-40°F/-40°C	15'–20' x 15'–20' (4.5–6 m x 4.5–6 m)	Partial Sun–Full Sun	October–December
Dogwood (silky)	Cornus amomum	-20°F/-29°C	6'–12' x 6'–12' (1.8–3.6 m x 1.8–3.6 m)	Full Sun–Partial Shade	May–June
Dusty zenobia 'Woodlander's Blue'	Zenobia pulverulenta 'Woodlander's Blue'	-10°F/-23°C	3'–10' x 2'–4' (0.9–3 m x 0.6–1.2 m)	Full Sun–Partial Shade	May
Dwarf fothergilla	Fothergilla gardenii	-20°F/-29°C	2'–4' x 2'–4' (0.6–1.2 m x 0.6–1.2 m)	Partial Shade–Full Sun	April–May
Ground-sel bush	Baccharis halimifolia	-20°F/-29°C	5'–12' x 5'–8' (1.5–3.6 m x 1.5–2.4 m)	Full Sun–Partial Shade	September–October
Inkberry holly	Ilex glabra	-30°F/-34°C	5'–8' x 5'–8' (1.5–2.4 m x 1.5–2.4 m)	Partial Shade–Full Sun	May–June
Ninebark	Physocarpus opulifolius	-50°F/-46°C	5'–8' x 5'–8' (1.5–2.4 m x 1.5–2.4 m)	Partial Shade–Full Sun	May–June
Purple-flowering raspberry	Rubus odoratus	-40°F/-40°C	3'–6' x 6'–12' (0.9–1.8 m x 1.8–3.6 m)	Partial Shade	June–August
Pussy willow	Salix discolor	-30°F/-34°C	6'–15' x 4'–12' (1.8–4.5 m x 1.2–3.6 m)	Full Sun–Partial Shade	March–April
(Red) Chokecherry	Aronia arbutifolia	-30°F/-34°C	6'–10' x 3'–6' (1.8–3 m x 0.9–1.8 m)	Full Sun–Partial Shade	April
Red twig dogwood	Cornus sericea	-40°F/-40°C	6'–9' x 7'–10' (1.8–2.7 m x 2.1–3 m)	Full Sun–Partial Shade	May–June
Smooth hydrangea	Hydrangea arborescens	-40°F/-40°C	3'–5' x 3'–5' (0.9–1.5 m x 0.9–1.5 m)	Partial Shade–Full Sun	June–September
Sweet pepperbush	Clethra alnifolia	-40°F/-40°C	3'–8' x 4'–6' (0.9–2.4 m x 1.2–1.8 m)	Partial Shade–Full Sun	July–August
Vernal witch hazel	Hamamelis vernalis	-30°F/-34°C	4'–10' x 8'–15' (1.2–3 m x 2.4–4.5 m)	Full Sun–Partial Shade	January–April
Virginia sweetspire	Itea virginica	-20°F/-29°C	3'–5' x 3'–5' (0.9–1.5 m x 0.9–1.5 m)	Full Sun–Partial Shade	June–July

OTHER CHARACTERISTICS	RAIN GARDEN	POND EDGE	RIPARIAN SLOPE	STREAM-SIDE	WET-LAND	SALT TOLERANT
Attracts birds and butterflies; juice and jam can be made from the berries and fritters from the flowers; fragrant	Yes	Yes	Yes	Yes	Yes	No
Attracts birds and butterflies; straight long stems; attractive leaf margins; wide range of fall color	No	Yes	Yes	Yes	Yes	No
Attracts birds; great fragrance to leaves and bark; waxy berries used for candle-making	No	No	Yes	Yes	Yes	Yes
Beautiful white flowers in spring with excellent fruiting in late summer for human and other animal consumption; plums make a great jam or pie; in blue-black or golden-yellow	Yes	Yes	Yes	Yes	Yes	Yes
Attracts birds; juice and jams can be made from the berries; yellow to orange fall color; suckers	No	No	Yes	Yes	Yes	Yes
Beautiful flowers that attracts a myriad of insects and hummingbirds; forms amazing stands	Yes	Yes	Yes	Yes	Yes	Yes
Beautiful flowers that attract many pollinators; fragrant; wonderful in mass	Yes	Yes	No	Yes	Yes	Yes
Great fragrance to leaves and bark; flowers have a spicy fragrance; excellent spreader by suckers	Yes	Yes	Yes	Yes	Yes	No
Flowers in late fall while leaves are a bright yellow; used for medicinal purposes; including skin rashes and irritations; nice fragrance	No	Yes	Yes	Yes	Yes	Yes
Has noticeably purple to plum colored stems when bare in the winter-time; attracts birds and pollinators; forms thickets; great for erosion control	Yes	Yes	Yes	Yes	Yes	Yes
The leaves are blue-green with a white underside; wonderful bell-shaped flowers in white	Yes	Yes	Yes	Yes	Yes	Yes
Planted in mass creates an amazing show, especially in the fall with colors ranging from yellow to orange to red	Yes	Yes	Yes	No	Yes	Yes
Beautiful white frothy flowers in the fall; tough plant along road ways where runoff is high; tolerates salt; plant is toxic to grazing animals; semi-evergreen to deciduous; can be weedy	No	Yes	Yes	Yes	Yes	Yes
Evergreen; species is usually bare on the lower half of plant; attracts birds and pollinators; berries used for ink; can spread by suckering; best used in mass; dioecious	No	No	Yes	Yes	Yes	Yes
Beautiful leaves with ornate lobed leaf margins; interesting capsules that persist over winter; flowers in profusion when planted in full sun; there are many new cultivars of this plant; yellow fall color; exfoliating bark	Yes	Yes	Yes	Yes	No	No
Leaf is attractive with five lobes; suckers to reproduce; fruits are edible; fragrant	No	Yes	Yes	Yes	Yes	Yes
Great for making waddles; baskets; riparian restoration; cut-flower market; roots very easily; great spring bloom sold for cutting; buy male plant for best catkin displays (dioecious)	Yes	Yes	Yes	No	Yes	Yes
Attracts birds; berries can be made into jam; too tart to eat fresh; great red fall color; berries are beautiful in winter; best used in mass	No	Yes	No	Yes	Yes	Yes
Attracts birds and butterflies; good fall color and nice blooms; best known for the red twigs in winter-time; twigs can be cut and sold for baskets; riparian restoration; cut-flower market; roots easily	No	Yes	Yes	Yes	Yes	Yes
Blooms on new wood; many new cultivars; faded blooms remain on plant during the winter months; looks great planted in mass; does best when pruned to the ground in spring	Yes	No	Yes	Yes	Yes	No
Attracts birds; pollinators including butterflies and hummingbirds; suckers; fragrant; yellow fall foliage; seed capsules remain during winter	Yes	Yes	Yes	No	Yes	Yes
Attracts pollinators and birds; great fragrance; suckers; yellow to gold fall color	No	Yes	No	Yes	No	No
Attracts pollinators and birds; great fragrance; suckers; red to yellow to orange fall color; seed capsules persist over winter; stems are green to red to gray-brown	Yes	No	No	Yes	Yes	Yes

Reproduction Strategies

There is a great diversity in the reproductive times of plants. Willow and other plant species living in wetland circumstances may asexually reproduce rapidly to gain control over fragile and shifting soils, or to compete with other plants for space and valuable resources. These plants allow for other plants to grow jointly as one plant community to decrease ecosystem movement and act as stabilizing agents for vast areas. If their mission in the environment is to stabilize a wetland, plants like these may reproduce more frequently via asexual propagation than from seed. And if the plant does reproduce from seed, it may have to have a seed that can float downstream to establish itself on the banks of the stream where there is nothing growing. The whole idea is to perpetuate the species somewhere else where there is no competition from itself. Bladdernut (*Staphylea trifolia*) is a good example, having fruit that floats and the ability to sucker, forming thickets.

◀ The bladder of bladdernut is airtight for floating downstream.

Additional Information on Hillsides and Steep Slopes

Tough and vigorous plants have growth habits that stabilize hillsides and steep slopes easily—after all, that's their job. I often hear people say that certain plants are too aggressive, or they seed in too much, but these comments seem to be missing the point. There are a great many habitats in our environment that are inhospitable and need aggressive plants to take charge. These shrubs act like the engineers of the plant world—constantly trying to stabilize themselves on precarious surfaces. They grow quickly and adjust their positions by sending out additional roots to stabilize the soil beneath and prevent rock falls, mudslides, and siltation. Aggression doesn't necessarily mean bad. It can be lifesaving, especially where unstable soils can cause road closures, flash flooding, and total inundation. The following chart shares details on some of my favorite shrubs for hillsides and slopes.

Shrubs for Steep Slopes and Hillsides

COMMON NAME	LATIN NAME	LOWEST HARDINESS TEMPERATURE	OVERALL SIZE (H×W)	BLOOM TIME	OTHER NOTABLE CHARACTERISTICS
Staghorn sumac 'Bailtiger' TIGER EYES®	*Rhus typhina* 'Bailtiger' TIGER EYES®	-20°F / -29°C	3'–6' × 3'–6' (0.9–1.8 m × 0.9–1.8 m)	Early Summer– June/July	Tough; quick to establish; can be planted in containers; good for erosion control; also does well in a garden bed; will not be as vibrant in color when planted in shade
Staghorn sumac 'Dissecta'	*Rhus typhina* 'Dissecta'	-30°F / -34°C	10'–25' × 15'–25' (3–7.6 × 4.5–7.6 m)	Early Summer– June/July	Lacy in appearance (almost fern-like); full sun to partial shade; can typically be found along riparian corridors; mowing near the roots will disturb their stability as sumac does not like soil compaction
Staghorn sumac	*Rhus typhina*	-30°F / -34°C	15'–25' × 20'–30' (4.5–7.6 × 6–9 m)	Early Summer– June/July	Pushes out undesirable weeds while keeping the soil beneath cool and moist; dioecious, with separate male and female plants; fruit on female staghorn sumac used as a spice in Middle Eastern cooking and by Native Americans to make vitamin C tea; color in fall is flame orange to fire-engine-red; has an enormous value for animal habitat, for numerous pollinators, and is a food source for birds; reproduces asexually from the roots by suckering
Fragrant sumac 'Gro-Low'	*Rhus aromatica* 'Gro-Low'	-30°F / -34°C	1½'–2' × 6'–8' (45–61 cm × 1.8–2.4)	March–April	Good for hedging; shrub groundcover that creates a thick mat, reducing maintenance on slopes; amazing fall color in yellows, oranges, and reds; short spring bulbs can be planted through it; dioecious
Winged sumac	*Rhus copallinum*	-20°F / -29°C	7'–15' × 10'–20' (2.1–4.5 × 3–6 m)	Late Spring–Early Summer	Creates walls of tall growth; panicles (or tassels of seed), when fruited, are ideal for attracting birds; male and female plants needed for fruiting; fruit can be used in cooking and for making tea; can be under-planted with spring bulbs and shade-loving perennials
Creeping raspberry	*Rubus calycinoides*	-0°F / -18°C	½' × 1½'–2' (15 × 45–61 cm)	Late Spring–Early Summer	Creates a luscious carpet of white flowers in the spring; enjoys heat, full sun, and good drainage; excellent for erosion control; berries are better for birds than humans; grows happily in dry shade; leaves are small and lobed
Winter jasmine	*Jasminum nudiflorum*	-30°F / -34°C	1½'–2' × 6'–8' 45–61 cm × 1.8–2.4 m	December– February	Green stems year-round; yellow tubular flowers begin to open sporadically; one of the only jasmines without a fragrance; asexually reproduces by layering along the ground; impenetrable layering habit means weeds have a hard time poking through; low maintenance; helps slow down water on slopes

The American bullfrog (*Lithobates catesbeianus* or *Rana catesbeiana*) enjoys the edges of ponds and rain gardens.

Ponds and Rain Gardens

Think of water as a resource—a commodity that you want to hold on to rather than get rid of. Rethink how we utilize our precious resources. Rain gardens and ponds hold excess water and turn it into a valuable commodity that can be used for irrigation, recreation, and habitat. Build it and they will come.

What do ponds and rain gardens have in common? They are passive destinations for water to coalesce. The water may move into these areas quickly, but the water stays on after a heavy rainfall. Plants that can tolerate standing water and water edges are excellent in these locations. In the case of the rain garden, the water will slowly percolate through the soil to the groundwater below, acting like a giant filter for cleansing the water before moving it through the system. Rain gardens prevent added pressure on storm drains for local municipalities and cities, which reduces the burden on infrastructure. Even personal properties have less pressure on infrastructure by having rain gardens. The gardens help to move water away from building foundations, reducing basement flooding.

Several rain gardens situated on a property can help redirect water away from the house and away from already burdened streams and riparian areas. And the best thing about rain gardens—they can be exceptionally attractive. Underground cisterns add additional storage for later water reuse.

Pond water, on the other hand, disappears through evapotranspiration and through seeps (small leaks or rills) that occur at the pond's edge and release water in very slow increments over time. The pond bottom is usually a water-holding substrate like a clay fragipan. A fragipan is an altered layer of soil that blocks water and roots from penetrating it. Plant roots may not be able to penetrate the fragipan, but they do play an important role in holding the pond's banks in place. Seeps may occur along the pond's edge, but they will be slowed by the plant community surrounding the pond.

Ponds are usually at low points on a property and buffering them along their edges helps prevent pollutants from entering the water. This is also true along streams, in riparian corridors, and in rain gardens. Planting buffers 50 to 75 feet (15.2 to 22.9 m) wide can reduce pollutants and sediment up to 80 percent—keeping all water features healthier, cleaner, and clearer.

There is a great deal to think about when planting around waterways, ponds, and rain gardens. The benefits that are gained lead to healthier, longer-lasting, and stable environments for animals—including humans.

When planting, be sure to have an open area to allow access to the water, not only for safety, but to enjoy the activity that your new landscape will afford. Make sure when designing your water areas that you have subshrubs as well as medium and taller plants. The variation in height will provide layers for animal cover and will create a great diversity in the water-edge habitat.

Another group of smaller water catchments are vernal pools that appear in spring and dry out later in the season. Vernal pools are depressions—typically in woodlands—that are critical habitat for amphibian life cycles. Many times, these depressions are filled in by well-meaning homeowners or land managers that don't know about their importance and function. Vernal pools act like mini ponds that completely evaporate—soaked up by shrubs and trees by season's end. They then fill again by the following spring, starting the cycle over again.

Shrubs and small tree groupings work well at pond and rain garden sites. Look at their overall size and light requirements before planting. Taking clues from nearby native habitats helps with the selection process and ties the surrounding plant communities to yours. Over time, ponds and rain gardens provide habitat and add to the seasonal vista changes. The blooms will bring in pollinators, while the fruits will bring in birds and other wildlife. Maintenance in these areas is typically reduced if the plants are installed properly. However, monitoring is an important aspect of water-feature plantings. Monitoring is observing how the plants are functioning and making sure a healthy layering system exists. If additional layers of shrubs are needed, they can be added through careful selection to promote balance within the new plant community you have established. Keeping good garden records helps decision-making for future additions.

If heavy deer browsing becomes an issue, select additional plants that are typically not browsed by deer, or select plants that benefit from browsing, like strawberry bush (*Euonymus americanus*). Similar to swamp titi mentioned in Chapter 9, strawberry bush, when browsed, sprouts from the roots from the hoof action of deer. Their hooves act like little plows, helping to loosen soil to allow new shoots to

▲ The male dabbling duck (*Anas platyrhynchos*) dances in his clean habitat.

◀ The green stems and strawberry-like fruit of the strawberry bush (*Euonymus americanus*) are ideal for visual interest around a pond, near a rain garden, or in a riparian area.

root systems to encourage faster growth. Smaller plants can be worked in between the larger ones to give faster cover.

If you want good views of the pond from the house or viewing area, plant shrubs that are not as tall in front of the pond. They will still give great cover and color. Taller shrubs can be situated toward the back of the pond, showing a progression in height.

On page 198, you can find a chart of several lower-statured plants that work well for the front of the pond.

When planting anything along water ways and ponds, try to plant with as little disturbance as possible by digging holes into lawns or bare soil and covering the area around and in between the plants with newspaper or cardboard—then mulch the plantings. To prevent contamination, do not use dyed mulch products near water features or waterways. Triple-ground hardwood mulch or thick layers of pine needles are ideal for this type of planting. The shrubs closest to the water feature should be planted closer together on 2-foot (61 cm) centers.

Quickly moving waterways need to be treated differently than placid ponds and rain gardens. Wider, more complex and layered green corridors are the most ideal for stream areas, especially at the headwaters of a stream. Habitat diversity is important in these areas to attract larger species.

sprout, creating thicker and lusher stands of the shrub. Strawberry bush's green stems allow the plant to photosynthesize in winter as well as the regular growing season, encouraging additional root growth and suckering.

The flowers on strawberry bush are small and fragrant but not showy. The strawberry-like fruits appear after the flowers are fertilized. Later, when the fruit is ripe, it splits open to reveal orange berries inside that are bold and beautiful against the pink outer coat. The leaves turn a handsome range of pink to orange to red in the fall, which adds to the plant's character.

Site strawberry bush ideally on the upper side of a rain garden or on a well-drained area near a pond. When trying to establish strawberry bush, it's best to get several larger plants with robust

Shrubs for Ponds and Rain Gardens

COMMON NAME	LATIN NAME	LOWEST HARDINESS TEMPERATURE	OVERALL SIZE (H×W)	BLOOM TIME	OTHER NOTABLE CHARACTERISTICS
Arrowwood viburnum	*Viburnum dentatum*	-40°F / -40°C	6'–10' × 6'–10' (1.8–3 m × 1.8–3 m)	Late May– Early June	In spring, clean white flowers and crisp-toothed leaves attract a diverse group of pollinators; berries attract a wide range of birds; plant along the pond edge or at the edge of a rain garden; little to no weeding necessary; long association with Native American tribes, who used the long stems to make shafts for arrows, hence its common name
Bigleaf hydrangea	*Hydrangea macrophylla*	-0°F / -18°C	3'–6' × 3'–6' (0.9–1.8 m × 0.9–1.8 m)	July–August	Flowers change color according to the pH of the soil—blue if the soil is acidic, pink if the soil is basic, and purple if the soil is neutral; the leaves make a delicious tea and persist through the winter months; plant along the pond edge or at the edge of a rain garden; little to no weeding necessary
Bottlebrush buckeye	*Aesculus parviflora*	-20°F / -29°C	8'–12' × 8'–15' (2.4–3.6 m × 2.4–4.5 m)	June–July	Has several strategies for reproduction—suckering and rapid seed germination; forms massive thickets that help prevent erosion; seeds root easily after falling to the ground; flowers attract various pollinators, including hummingbirds; bright gold color in fall; flowers sit above the foliage like a halo
Buttonbush	*Cephalanthus occidentalis*	-10°F / -23°C	5'–12' × 4'–8' (1.5–3.6 m × 1.2–2.4 m)	June– September	Produces a button-like fruit or an aggregate of achenes (the seeds), which readily propagate without any treatments; a pollinator magnet; good for around ponds, in rain gardens, wetlands, and along streams; can tolerate standing water and help stabilize wetlands and fragile edge areas
Dusty zenobia 'Woodlander's Blue'	*Zenobia pulverulenta* 'Woodlander's Blue'	-10°F / -23°C	2'–4' × 3'–4' (0.6–1.2 m × 0.9–1.2 m)	May–June	Underutilized and underappreciated, but very attractive; small white bell-shaped flowers followed by upward-facing seed capsules; unique blue-green-colored foliage; prefers sandy, acidic soils near ponds, creeks, and damp habitats; can handle sun as well as partial shade to provide effective blooms; cultivar released by Woodlanders Nursery, Aiken, South Carolina
Silky dogwood	*Cornus amomum*	-10°F / -23°C	6'–12' × 6'–12' (1.8–3.6 m × 1.8–3.6 m)	May–June	Typically found in sodden soils or areas where there is downspout runoff; forms massive colonies, contributing to food sources for pollinators and birds; ability to adventitiously root; plum-colored stems in winter; one of the top plant engineers for securing stream banks; can tolerate standing water

COMMON NAME	LATIN NAME	LOWEST HARDINESS TEMPERATURE	OVERALL SIZE (H×W)	BLOOM TIME	OTHER NOTABLE CHARACTERISTICS
Smooth witherod 'Winterthur'	*Viburnum nudum* 'Winterthur'	-10°F / -23°C	5'–12' × 5'–12' (1.5–3.6 m × 1.5–3.6 m)	April–May	Amazing fall color and beautiful berries; plant along the pond edge or at the edge of a rain garden; little to no weeding necessary
Sweet pepperbush 'Hummingbird'	*Clethra alnifolia* 'Hummingbird'	-30°F / -34°C	2'–4' × 3'–5' (0.6–1.2 m × 0.9–1.5 m)	July–August	Low profile looks neat and clean with mass planting; plant along a pond, in a rain garden, and along streams; amazing fragrance; hummingbirds, butterflies, and an array of pollinators are attracted to the plant
Sweet pepperbush 'Rosea'	*Clethra alnifolia* 'Rosea'	-20°F / -29°C	3'–6' × 3'–5' (0.9–1.8 m × 0.9–1.5 m)	July–August	Pale-pink form; can be planted in shady areas as well as sunny locations if in moist or wet soils
Sweet pepperbush 'Ruby Spice'	*Clethra alnifolia* 'Ruby Spice'	-20°F / -29°C	4'–6' × 3'–5' (1.2–1.8 m × 0.9–1.5 m)	July–August	Has a taller stature similar to the species but is more consistent in growth habit; clear pink flowers with a spicy fragrance; can be planted in shady areas as well as sunny locations if in moist or wet soils
Winterberry	*Ilex verticillata*	-30°F / -34°C	3'–12' × 3'–12' (0.9–3.6 m × 0.9–3.6 m)	June–July	Heavy berry production great for bird watching; can be planted directly into a rain garden or along the edge of a pond
Winterberry 'Winter Gold'	*Ilex verticillata* 'Winter Gold'	-30°F / -34°C	5'–8' × 5'–8' (1.5–2.4 m × 1.5–2.4 m)	May–June	Has long-lasting berries that add warmth to the landscape in winter; cut stems are ideal for floral arranging
Virginia sweetspire	*Itea virginica*	-10°F / -23°C	3'–5' × 3'–5' (0.9–1.5 m × 0.9–1.5 m)	June–July	Taller version of 'Henry's Garnet'; growth is not as consistent and can get rangy with age; performs best in full sun, providing blankets of flowers; does well in shade but will not yield as many flowers; has a sweet fragrance
Virginia sweetspire 'Henry's Garnet'	*Itea virginica* 'Henry's Garnet'	-10°F / -23°C	3'–4' × 4'–6' (0.9–1.2 m × 1.2–1.8 m)	May–June	Works well on steep slopes or flat areas; plant well-established specimens on 3-foot (0.9 m) centers with a staggered planting pattern to slow water going into the waterway; within a year or two there will be complete cover with shrubs forming a massive thicket with intertwining root; can handle wet feet

Salty Environments

Ditches and drainage channels along road-ways where there are no curbs or sidewalks benefit from planting salt-tolerant plants, especially after a long winter of snow, ice, and applications of deicing salts. Salt buildup in these areas creates a beach-like environment, calling for heavy-hitting salt-loving plants to clean and stabilize the sites. Bayberry is a tenacious plant that has thick, shiny leaf surfaces to keep the plant from desiccating. The plant may be evergreen, semi-evergreen, or deciduous depending on the winter weather. When you break a stem or remove leaves from the plant, the fragrance tells you that it's in the myrtle family (Myrtaceae). The low wide stature of bayberry takes a prominent

position on the sand dunes with beach plum. I can't imagine our landscapes without it. Site the shrub along pathways that are salted in winter, and use as a highway planting on any steep embankment. The berries are an important part of migratory flyway food, and the plant creates protective cover during coastal storms.

Candleberry is the southern version of the northern bayberry. The myrtle warbler (*Setophaga coronata* var. *coronata*) gets its name from its close association with the plant. The waxy berries are used to make candles—the well-known Williamsburg signature. The leaves on candleberry are narrower than bayberry and have golden glands on the underside, making the two plants more easily identified. Both

Right: Beach plums are great soil stabilizers and are salt tolerant. In August, the plants are full of luscious plums for wildlife and to make jellies and jams.

Far right, top: The lush green foliage of candleberry makes a wonderful backdrop for a perennial border. Candleberry can also be used as a foundation plant or a screen. It makes a nice cozy alleé too!

Far right, bottom: Sweet fern—with leaves resembling a fern—gives a delicate and fine appearance in the garden.

Plants for Salty Environments

Beach plum (*Prunus maritima*) (-30°F 3'–6' × 3'–6')
   (34°C 0.9–1.8 m x 0.9–1.8 m)
Bayberry (*Myrica pensylvanica*) (-10°F 6'–12' × 6'–12')
   (-23°C 1.8–3.6 m x 1.8–3.6 m)
Candleberry (*Morella cerifera*) (-10°F 6'–12' × 6'–12')
   (-23°C 1.8–3.6 m x 1.8–3.6 m)
Eastern red cedar (*Juniperus virginiana*) (-40°F 30'–65' × 8'–25')
   (-40°C 9.1–20 m x 2.4–7.6 m)
Sweet fern (*Comptonia peregrina*) (-40°F 2'–5' × 4'–8')
   (-40°C 0.6–1.5 m x 1.2–2.4 m)
Groundsel bush (*Baccharis halimifolia*) (-10°F 5'–12')
   (-23°C 1.5–3.6 m)

bayberry and candleberry can be used as a wonderful hedge along roadways to protect salt-intolerant plants within the garden. Candleberry also has medicinal attributes: It's used as a gargle for scratchy throats and for sore gums.

Sweet fern, although not an actual fern, has a finer texture than other shrubs. When brushed through the hands, sweet fern has a wonderful, sweet, musty fragrance. It does well in low spots and looks tidy along walkways. Consider sweet fern for a mixed border or entryway because of its low stature.

The groundsel bush is a tough plant that has a fluffy bloom. In late fall the tiny seeds fly around like feathers and germinate without treatment. Thick waxy leaves make the plant tough along coastlines. In a garden setting, the fall bloom is a show-stopper. It too can be used as a hedge along roadways where other plants may not grow with excessive salt.

Examine the chart on page 190 for more ideas on salt-tolerant plants to include in salty areas. The column on the chart that indicates salt tolerance can help you select plants that are fantastic along roadways where heavy salt use is inevitable during major snowstorms and icy episodes.

Doing Our Part

As our earth's climate continues to change, we need to be mindful of our importance in the climate equation. Understanding our part to help vulnerable and fragile land is the first step to building better landscapes that will multiply in benefits over time. If we critically think about our contributions, we can understand the interconnectivity to the larger ecosystem that is our earth home.

For a long time, people gardened in isolation with the idea that what they did on their properties didn't matter to the rest of the world. But I am here to remind you that everything we do does matter. Good stewardship on our properties equates to high-functioning ecosystems. Holding each other accountable ensures our larger environmental communities will be healthier and less vulnerable to pollution and habitat loss. This is not a dream—it's the new reality!

CHAPTER 11

HOW, WHEN, AND WHERE TO PURCHASE SHRUBS

Selecting plants at retailers can be daunting. How do you know what traits to look for and which plants will be best for your landscape? This chapter walks you through the ins and outs of shopping for shrubs.

How to Choose the Right Shrubs

There are numerous points to consider when buying new shrubs for your yard and garden. First, look for a plant that will physically fit the site. Measure the site before you shop so you don't buy too many plants for the area or plants of the wrong size. Check the plant's tag or ask a sales associate at the garden center to make sure the mature growth dimensions of the shrub are similar to the space you have available for it. Selecting the right plant for the right place reduces overall maintenance and increases your enjoyment of the plant. Pruning should be done only when necessary.

Consider the lighting conditions of the area. Observe your garden's light conditions before purchasing shrubs to create the best results.

Also consider the shrub's bloom time. Plant retailers tend to sell more plants when they are in bloom. After all, the easiest way for the buyer to see the color of the bloom and get the full impact of the plant is to see it when it's in bloom.

Before You Purchase Shrubs

Not being prepared for selecting plants can cause impulsive buying. This typically means over-purchasing and winding up with plants that are pretty in bloom from the garden center but don't have the proper environment in your garden to bloom again the same way. Having the best possible environment for the plants you are purchasing will lead to endless joy each time you are in your garden. Here are some valuable points to consider before purchasing in order to get the gorgeous garden you desire.

1) Testing Your Soil

A soil test will help you determine if your soil has any nutrient deficiencies, while also providing you with the pH of your soil. Lower pH soils that are below 6 can support a host of ericaceous (acid-loving) plants. Rhododendrons, azaleas, blueberries, mountain laurel, and so on will do beautifully. A pH between 6.5 and 7 is classified as neutral and is ideal for a huge range of plants. Soils that have a pH of 7 or higher are considered basic or alkaline. Willows are

Garden centers offer a wide selection of plants while providing high-quality service. A sea of evergreens gives clients a vast selection.

a good example of plants that can tolerate basic soil without any problems.

The soil test should also tell you if your soil needs any amendments. Adding the recommended elements will help to balance the nutrient content of your soil, which leads to healthier growth. Without having basic knowledge ahead of time, you may be purchasing plants that won't work for your site.

Soil testing kits can be purchased through your local cooperative extension. Almost every state in the United States has a university that tests soils. Google "cooperative extension" and the name of your state, and your cooperative extension school should pop up. If you don't take that route, you can use a commercial entity to test your soil. If you are still uncertain about soil testing, your local garden center can also direct you.

There is also another test that you can do on your own to determine the friability of your soil (how well it crumbles). Take a handful of soil and squeeze it in your hand. If the soil is slippery and forms a mass, your soil probably has a high clay content. If you squeeze the soil and some of it forms lumps but some falls apart, you may have a clay loam. If you look at the chart below, the soil that has the least aggregation is sand—it runs right through the fingers. Testing soil like this helps you to understand the makeup of the soil you will be dealing with. Soils with high clay content benefit from mixing in compost to loosen the soil and allow more air spaces between the clay particles.

Another test that you can do is dig a hole and then pour a bucket of water into the hole. Time how long it takes for the water to drain from the hole. If it passes through quickly, you have a higher macropore space (air spaces), which means you have larger soil particle size—more sand than clay. If it takes several hours to drain, then you are dealing with a high clay content.

The length of percolation time will determine what type of plants can tolerate your soil. Slower-draining soils are ideal for wetland plants, while faster-draining soils are more suitable for upland species. There is also a range of exceedingly adaptable plants that can go from one extreme to the other without any problems.

2) Creating a Design and Selecting Plant Sizes

Do you have a design for the area that you are planting? If not, come up with a quick sketch of the area and where you think you would like plants, noting the height of plants that will work best. Chapter 5 can

The soil pyramid helps to determine the texture of your soil. There are many combinations of the three main soil types of sand, silt, and clay.

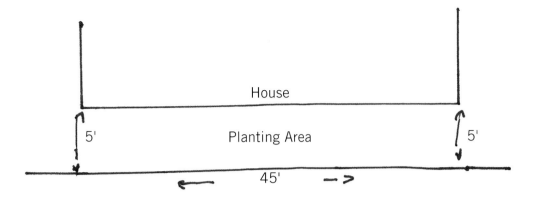

Quick sketch with dimensions for plant purchase

give you some ideas on how to approach your design. Your design will assist in making your shopping easier.

Measuring the dimensions will determine the number of plants for the area. Once you get to the garden center you can check the plant tags to make sure the dimensions listed are similar to or smaller than what you planned to purchase. Sometimes the label can underestimate the size of a plant. The sizes listed are averages, not exact measurements, because every site influences a plant's growth differently. If you have an ideal spot for the plant, it may get bigger than the tag's estimates.

Developing one area at a time in your garden will keep you from getting overwhelmed. Tackle areas that you feel are the most critical for your visual enjoyment as you come and go from your home each day. The first garden area that you complete will give you a feeling of satisfaction that will encourage other new garden areas.

By selecting the right plant for the right place, you reduce overall maintenance and increase your enjoyment of the garden. Pruning should be done only when necessary, and remember the three Ds. (See Chapter 6 on pruning.)

3) Lighting

Consider the lighting conditions that you have in your garden. You can make a little chart of where the sun rises and sets in your landscape. If the plant requires full sun, a location that receives 6 hours or more of sunlight daily is needed for the plant to perform at its best. If the plant's tag says the shrub prefers partial sun or partial shade, between 4 and 6 hours of sunlight a day will suffice. A shrub that requires partial shade could also be happy in the dappled shade beneath the leaf canopy of a larger tree. Watch the shadows on the ground under the tree to confirm that there is scattered light beneath. Some trees do not allow any light to pass through the leaf canopy. If this is the case, a site like this would be considered full shade. Other full-shade conditions, such as those on the north side of a building, receive only limited reflected sun. Observing your garden's lighting conditions before you purchase will prevent any casualties over time.

Once you have all the data collected from your garden, you are ready to shop. It's best not to go blindly into any garden center or nursery without having your sketch and a list of the plants that you will

Right: Mapleleaf viburnum has great fall color even in deep shade.

Bottom left: Deutzia 'Nikko' will fill the light-shade area of 8' × 8' (2.4 × 2.4 m).

Bottom right: Sweet box has a great late-winter fragrance when in bloom and stays evergreen. It grows well in deep shade.

need. Just like cooking, you want to know all the ingredients for your recipe before you go grocery shopping. Here is what your garden list should look like:

- Shrubs that will be a good groundcover (all the same type)—for light shade but sunny in spring—area 8' × 8' (2.4 × 2.4 m)—soil pH is neutral to slightly acidic—approximate height of plants desired is 2' (61 cm)—something that blooms in spring. I like the way deutzia 'Nikko' (*Deutzia gracilis* 'Nikko') (-10°F 1'–2' × 2'–5') (-23°C 30–61 cm × 61–152 cm) looks as a groundcover, and the measurements fit the requirements for this area.

- Shrubs (several types) for a spot that is a shady, but is sunny in spring—area 10' × 5' (3 × 1.5 m)—pH same as above—approximate height 4' to 6' (1.2 to 1.8 m) or can be shorter, but the width should not be more than 4' (1.2 m). Here I might select mapleleaf viburnum (*Viburnum acerifolium*) (-30°F 3'–6' ×

2'–4') (-34°C 0.9–1.8 m × 61–120 cm) and underplant it with sweet box (*Sarcococca hookeriana* var. *humilis*) (-0°F 1'–2' × 2'–4') (-18°C 30–61 cm × 61–120 cm).

Deutzia 'Nikko' has dainty white flowers in spring and a beautiful melon to orange fall color.

The overhang (pergola) is providing partial shade for hydrangea and other plants that require it. Primex Garden Center in Glenside, Pennsylvania.

Blue-black berries and white spring flowers add to the seasonal interest of mapleleaf viburnum.

Buy by Bloom

Nurseries, garden centers, and big-box stores typically sell plants when they are in bud and bloom. It's the easiest way for a gardener to see the color of the bloom and its full impact. It's also a great way to select color combinations. You can take a few different plants and put them side by side to see how they look together. Is there diversity in the look and feel? Are there nice contrasts?

Retail outlets typically keep shrubs in the conditions they require. Note how and where they are displayed. Shade-loving plants are usually under a shade cloth or protected by an overhang. Pay attention to these kinds of details; they can help you find the best plant for your site.

Helpful Staff

Asking trained staff for help is a way to learn more about the plants that you are considering. Learn which stores have the best staff for advice, and save a great deal of time and money in the long run. Having well-trained staff shows that the store is professional. They are not just selling plants, they are there for you with gardening expertise. Plants may cost a bit more, but the cost is certainly worth the professional advice. Buying cheaper plants elsewhere can mean spending more money in the long run because you bought the wrong plants. Professional private retailers usually go the extra mile for their clients because they want to have life-long relationships with gardening residents in their communities. Having a good rapport with garden centers and nurseries will also keep you abreast of what's new in the gardening world and what problems may be plaguing an area (e.g., spotted

Surreybrooke Nursery in Middletown, Maryland, shows clients how the shrubs look when planted in their landscape.

lanternfly, viburnum leaf beetle, and emerald ash borer). Many garden centers offer classes to assist their clients with additional information.

Keep Going Back for More

Purchasing throughout the growing season can be a big help with budgeting. Keep notes about what appeals to you at the garden center. In case your budget doesn't allow for an immediate purchase, you can come back when the plants are on sale or come back the following year.

Visit your favorite stores several times during the growing season to check out the shrubs that are blooming. If there's a time in your garden that nothing is in bloom, that's the time to visit a nursery or garden center. Retailers restock their inventories every week or every few weeks during the growing season. By purchasing plants in this manner, you will be spacing out bloom times in your garden. Ideally, you should have something in bloom from late winter all the way until heavy frost for maximum enjoyment and curb appeal. Remember, curb appeal is not just for others to see, it's for you to enjoy each time you arrive home and spend time in the garden.

Having plants blooming in every month also ensures pollinator activity in the garden. If you have a vast array of plants in your landscape, you'll have a diversity of pollinators, followed by birds, bats, and other predators that will make a healthier environment.

Signage and Plant Tags

When looking for a specific characteristic of a plant, look to the signage at the nursery or retail outlet. Many stores will have plants grouped by their function, with signs that read "pollinator plants," "shade-loving plants," "rain garden plants," etc.

When a new shrub is released, companies spend thousands of dollars on making the perfect plant tag to ensure that the consumer is well informed. A picture of the plant in bloom usually accompanies the specifications on the tag, just in case the plant isn't in bloom at the time of purchase. Other information that might appear on the label consists of the following:

- Lighting requirements
- USDA hardiness zones
- Height and width
- Planting distance between each plant
- Bloom time
- Soil and moisture requirements
- Soil pH—especially if the plant needs a lower pH
- Uses
- Instructions on how to plant your new shrub

Plant tags are user friendly and impart a range of information on a pocket-sized document. Websites are also listed for more in-depth information. The tags can be easily stored by the gardener for future reference after the shrub has been planted. Having a detailed log of where the plant was purchased, when the plant was purchased, and where it is located in the garden benefits the gardener over time. Some shrubs will perform very well, but others may die off or look sickly. Taking your own photos can show the progress or the deterioration of a plant.

Look at How the Plant Is Packaged

There are different ways to buy your plants—in containers (plastic or cloth), balled and burlapped (B&B), and sometimes bare root. Roses are often sold bare root in early spring before the plant breaks bud. There is a short window of opportunity for planting bare-root plants, but the results are excellent if they are properly cared for after purchase. Usually a good soaking before planting is required—the soaking gets the plant off to a great start.

Container-grown plants are easy to handle. They pack easily in cars, and plants can be purchased in varying sizes depending on budget. Some gardeners prefer to buy smaller plants and let them grow into place, while others prefer a much larger plant to fill a spot quickly. There is no right or wrong when making a purchase, just different preferences and budgets. When taking the plants out of the container, be sure to loosen up the roots if they are bound tight in the pot. Any circling roots should be cut to prevent further circling or girdling.

B&B plants are dug from the nursery and placed in burlap. Then the plant is placed into a wire cage that secures the burlap in place. The size of a B&B plant is usually much bigger than other plants, although there are some huge pot-grown specimens. B&B usually takes several people to maneuver the plant when not using a front-end loader. These plants typically have 70 percent less root systems after they are dug from the field, which makes regular watering crucial and takes plants longer to establish. When planting B&B plants, the wire cage should be removed before placing the plant in the planting hole. Burlap and strings should all be undone and removed.

Creating a Rapport

Developing a trusted source of suppliers can be an added value for the consumer. I love the fact that I can call my local garden center and ask for availability on a plant or group of plants. If they have what I want, they can pull the plants and set them aside for later pickup. If purchasing large orders, I can call ahead and have the order ready and waiting, or I can have it delivered. The latter saves valuable gardening time.

Consider going to the nursery or garden center on weekdays to find an employee who can give you more assistance. Having a great rapport with the garden center or nursery also helps to establish an account for valued discounts throughout the year.

Big-box stores typically do not provide the services independent garden centers and nurseries provide, because they are trying to sell the plants at the lowest possible prices. Service is not always their priority, although some are getting better at it.

Nurseries and Specialty Growers

There are nursery operations that just sell wholesale to retailers, nursery/garden center combos that sell wholesale and retail, and regular independent garden centers. The latter relies solely on plants that are available in the marketplace and are brought on site. Big-box stores bring plants in each year and try to sell out of everything in the stockyard by the end of the season, eliminating holdovers. Garden centers may have some plants as holdovers and give reasonable discounts come spring

or late fall. Nurseries that grow their plants can sell their plants throughout the year or as long as the weather is good for planting. They propagate their plants by making cuttings of their stock plants or purchasing woody cuttings to root. They may even start many plants from seed. If a plant starts to lose momentum in the marketplace, the number of plants being propagated may drop. The volume of sales sets the propagation numbers for the nursery.

Other nurseries and garden centers are specialty operations that carry plants no one else carries (e.g., heritage roses, specific native plants, or wetland plants). Their propagation methods vary depending on the plant.

Mail-Order Shipping

Purchasing through mail order is another good option. Plants can be shipped across the country as long as there are no restrictions through the Department of Agriculture. Ordering from a company website is ideal for the hard-to-find plant, or for smaller shipments of plants and bare-root specimens. Green industry professionals take pride in their quick delivery and expert packaging. I have received many plants through delivery services, and I am always amazed at how beautifully they are packaged. An incredible amount of work and dedication goes into the shipping process. The plants arrive in superior condition, usually ready to be planted. Sometimes they come with special instructions on what do with the plants once the package has been opened. Speaking of which, plants should be opened immediately upon arrival, even if you can't get to planting them right away. Getting into the open air

Japanese plum yew (*Cephalotaxus harringtonia* 'Duke Gardens') grows in part shade to full shade and is deer resistant. Meadowbrook Farm, Meadowbrook, Pennsylvania.

and light will reduce stress on the plants after being boxed for several days.

On company websites you can find the actual shipping dates—not all plants can be shipped when they are ordered. Your growing zone will determine when the plants are shipped. There are specific shipping times to ensure that each plant arrives in the best possible condition.

Be sure to time deliveries with your schedule. The last thing you want is a big box on your front doorstep sitting in the hot sun or the rain. You can even prepare the planting beds ahead of time. When the plants arrive, your task will be much easier. Remember to open the boxes as soon as they arrive.

Other Places to Purchase

Arboreta and botanic gardens hold plant sales in the spring and fall, and some even sell year-round because they have propagation programs. They may sell plants because they are being taught in their continuing education courses or because the botanic garden is known for a specific group of plants that are their hallmark. During special seasonal sales, plants are brought in from far and wide to give members and visitors another opportunity to purchase rare or hard-to-find varieties. They will often try to have newer varieties that have yet to hit the regular market. Many gardeners benefit from these special sales while also supporting their local arboretum or botanic garden.

Purchasing plants is easier than ever. As you continue to build your garden paradise, keep in mind how amazing gardening can be for improved health and enjoyment. You will make new friends along the journey as you continue to build your garden, knowing that your next new plant is a short drive or the press of a button away.

RESOURCES

Books

A Modern Herbal. Grieve, 1984.

American Botanical Paintings: Native Plants of the Mid Atlantic. Bonnie S. Driggers, Ed., 2012.

The Complete Book of Shrubs. Kim Tripp and Allen Coombes, 1998.

Culpeper's Complete Herbal and English Physician Enlarged. N. Culpeper, 1990.

Edible Wild Plants Eastern/Central North America. Lee Allen Peterson, 1977.

Flowering Trees and Shrubs: Biltmore Nursery. Biltmore, North Carolina, 1909.

Flowers for All Seasons. Jeff and Marilyn Cox, 1987.

Frontier Medicine from the Atlantic to the Pacific 1492-1941. David Dary, 2008.

Garden Shrubs and Their Histories. Alice Coats, 1992.

The Gossler Guide to the Best Hardy Shrubs. Rodger Gossler, Eric Gossler, and Marjory Gossler, 2009.

Hedge Britannia: A Curious History of a British Obsession. Hugh Barker, 2012.

The Journals of Lewis and Clark. Bernard DeVoto, (Ed), 1953.

Manual of Woody Landscape Plants, 6th Ed. Michael Dirr, 2009.

National Audubon Society Field Guide to North American Butterflies. Robert Michael Pyle, 1995.

Native Plants of the Northeast: A Guide for Gardening and Conservation. Donald J. Leopold, 2005.

The Natural Habitat Garden. Ken Druse, 2004.

The Plants of Pennsylvania, 2nd Ed. Ann Fowler Rhoads and Timothy A. Block, 2007.

Pollinators of Native Plants. Heather Holm, 2014.

The Reference Manual of Woody Plant Propagation: From Seed to Tissue Culture, 2nd Ed. Michael Dirr and Charles W. Heuser, Jr., 2006.

Topiary and Ornamental Hedges. Miles Hadfield, 1971.

Travels through North and South Carolina, Georgia, East and West Florida & Travels in Georgia and Florida 1773-1774. William Bartram, 1996.

Woody Cut Stems for Growers and Florists. Lane Greer and John Dole, 2009.

The Xerces Society Guide: Attracting Native Pollinators. 2011.

Websites
BEES
A View of Bees
www.beescape.org

Bee Informed
www.beeinformed.org

BIRDS

Audubon—Bird Flyways
www.audubon.org

Birdlife International—Migratory Birds
www.birdlife.org

PLANTS AND FLOWERS

American Conifer Society
www.conifersociety.org

The American Rhododendron Society
www.rhododendron.org

American Rose Society
www.rose.org

Aronia
www.aroniapoland.com

Bloomin' Easy®
www.bloomineasyplants.com

Easy Elegance® Roses
www.easyeleganceroses.com

Encore® Azaleas
www.encoreazalea.com

Endless Summer® Blooms
www.endlesssummerblooms.com

English Hedges. David Ross. Ed.
www.britainexpress.com

First Edition® Shrubs
www.baileynurseries.com/brands/first-editions

Flower Carpet®
www.tesselaar.com/plants/flower-carpet-roses

Holly Society of America
www.hollysocam.org

Instant Hedge™
www.instanthedge.com

Illinois Wildflowers
www.illinoiswildflowers.info

Oso Easy® Roses
www.provenwinners.com/plants/series/oso-easy

Plants for a Future
www.pfaf.org

Star Roses® and Plants—Ball Horticulture
www.starrosesandplants.com

BOTANIC GARDENS AND LIBRARIES

The Arnold Arboretum of Harvard University
www.arboretum.harvard.edu

Center for Pollinator Research
www.roserosette.org

Chicago Botanic Garden Plant Information
www.chicagobotanic.org

Commission for Environmental Cooperation
www.cec.org

Georgia Gold Medal Plant Program
www.botgarden.uga.edu

Lady Bird Johnson Wildflower Center
www.wildflower.org

Mt. Cuba Center
www.mtcubacenter.org

Missouri Botanic Garden Plant Finder Profile
www.missouribotanicalgarden.org

New York City Parks—Greenbelt Native
Plant Center
www.nycgovparks.org

Northern Prairie Wildlife Research Center
www.usgs.gov/centers/npwrc

Pennsylvania Horticultural Society—
Gold Medal Plant Program
www.phsonline.org

Smithsonian Tropical Research Herbarium
https://biogeodb.stri.si.edu/herbarium/

Thomas Jefferson's Monticello—Lucy
Meriwether Lewis Marks Collection
www.monticello.org

U Mass Extension—Landscape Fact Sheets
www.umass.edu

JOURNALS, DATABASES, AND OTHER USEFUL TOOLS

Find a Plant
www.plants.ces.ncsu.edu/find_a_plant

Floridata Master Plant List
www.floridata.com/plants/all

International Code of Botanical Nomenclature
www.biocyclopedia.com/index/icbn.php

International Code of Nomenclature for
Cultivated Plants
www.ishs.org/sites/default/files/static/
ScriptaHorticulturae_18.pdf

Journal of the American Rhododendron
Society
www.rhododendron.org/journal

Native American Ethnobotany
http://naeb.brit.org

Stihl Manual on Chainsaw Safety
www.stihl.com/p/media/download/uk-en/
STIHL_Chain_Saw_Safety_Manual.pdf

U.S. Forestry Service Native Plant Alternatives
www.fs.fed.us

USDA Hardiness Zone Map
https://planthardiness.ars.usda.gov/
PHZMWeb/

USDA Plants Database
https://plants.usda.gov/java/factSheet

Sources to Purchase Plants and Tools

A.M. Leonard Horticultural Tool & Supply
Company
www.amleo.com

Anthony Tesselaar Plants
https://tesselaar.com/plants

Ball Horticulture
www.ballhort.com

Bailey Nurseries
www.baileynurseries.com

Brotzman's Nursery
www.brotzmansnursery.com

California Native Plants and Habitat
Enhancement Services
www.watershednursery.com

Collins Nursery
www.collinsnursery.com

Grow Native—Missouri Prairie Foundation™
http://grownative.org/resource-guide/
shrubs-and-trees

Harmony Hill Nursery (for the trade only)
www.facebook.com/eatsleeptrees

Monrovia
www.monrovia.com/plant-catalog

Octoraro Native Plant Nursery
(for the trade only)
www.octoraro.com

Plant Native
www.plantnative.org/nd_ca.htm

Pleasant Run Nursery
www.pleasantrunnursery.com

Proven Winner Plants
www.provenwinners.com/plants

Sam Browns Wholesale Nursery
(for the trade only)
www.sambrownsnursery.com

Vanbelle
https://vanbelle.com

Woodlanders, Inc.
www.woodlanders.net

ACKNOWLEDGMENTS

It takes a village to write a book—especially in the early stages of development, when searching for information in libraries and archives. I could not have tackled this book without the help of the Longwood Gardens library staff: Gillian Hayward, Sandy Reber, Maureen McCadden, David Sleasman, and Jessica Kincaid. And the wonderful plant records manager, Kristina Aguilar, and my woody plants lab instructor, Virginia Levy. Additional thanks to other staff members at Longwood Gardens: Lori Harrison, Matthew Ross, Julie Bodenstab, Nancy Sharp, Susan Nichols, and Danilo Maffei.

I am grateful for those in the industry who supported my work and did preliminary advising: Stephanie Cohen, Teresa Woodard, Sarah Monheim, Denise Gilchrist, Cindy Ahern, and Terry Donahue. Thank you to Tom Horn and the staff at Primex Garden Center for their support. And thanks to Louise Clarke for the tool photos and to Thu Ngan Han for posing in the tool cleaning photo. Nursery people like Tim Brotzman of Brotzman's Nursery gave me insight into the nursery industry and its rich history through catalogue documentation. Patrick Mitchell and Christopher Uhland of Harmony Hill Nursery took the time to share their knowledge while I visited their nursery. And thanks also to Kevin Cramer at Vanbelle.

The team at Spring Meadow Nursery was supportive in my plant research. Natalie Carmolli, Diane Fullerton, and Stacey Hirvela: Thank you for showing me the latest in the industry. And many thanks to Dale and Liz Deppe for hosting me at their beautiful property, where additional photos were taken.

When I asked my colleagues from Garden Communicators International (GardenComm) for their favorite shrubs, they came through with a lengthy list of plants that supported my list of tried-and-true performers. Thank you!

A huge thank you to Karen Steenhoudt, colleague and former student, for her designs, along with Sue Mrugal and Gregg Tepper, both of whom are plants people extraordinaires.

Finally, I would like to thank the amazing staff at The Quarto Group and Cool Springs Press who guided the process of writing and editing: Jessica Walliser, Heather Godin, Meredith Quinn, and all the departments that make a book come to life and get into readers' hands. That's you, Steve Roth and Theodore Evans. Thank you!

ABOUT THE AUTHOR

Eva Monheim is an award-winning educator in horticulture with over thirty years of teaching to her credit. Currently, she teaches at Longwood Gardens for the Professional Horticulture Program and is a faculty member at The Barnes Arboretum of St. Joseph's University. Eva's early childhood experiences spending hours outdoors led to her passion for horticulture. A graduate of Penn State University and Arcadia University, and an alumna of the University of Reading in England, Eva holds degrees in horticulture, art, and English literature. Her education in England has given her a global appreciation of garden design and environmental sensitivity. Her accomplishments include being a certified arborist, master floral designer, artist, writer, and mentor. She is a member of the International Dendrology Society (IDS), International Society of Arboriculture (ISA), American Horticultural Society (AHS), Pennsylvania Horticultural Society (PHS), The Hardy Plant Society/ Mid-Atlantic Group, Women in Horticulture, GardenComm (Garden Communicators International), and an advocate for the Urban Wood Network. Eva's articles, designs, and photographs have appeared in national, regional, and local magazines and newspapers. Eva was an assistant professor at Temple University in the department of

landscape architecture and horticulture for over twelve years where she taught thirteen different subjects in undergraduate and graduate programs and was an early adaptor of teaching online. Eva has owned several businesses, including a flower shop and a landscaping company, and she is a principal at VEE—Verdant Earth Educators, LLC. Her breadth of knowledge in the industry is vast, which is evident in the classroom and in her writings. Eva's extensive teaching experience has empowered hundreds of students who are now leaders in the commercial and public sectors of the green industry and beyond.

INDEX